Rogue Nation

Books by Vernon Coleman

The Medicine Men (1975)
Paper Doctors (1976)
Everything You Want To Know About Ageing (1976)
Stress Control (1978)
The Home Pharmacy (1980)
Aspirin or Ambulance (1980)
Face Values (1981)
Guilt (1982)
The Good Medicine Guide (1982)
Stress And Your Stomach (1983)
Bodypower (1983)
An A to Z Of Women's Problems (1984)
Bodysense (1984)
Taking Care Of Your Skin (1984)
A Guide to Child Health (1984)
Life Without Tranquillisers (1985)
Diabetes (1985)
Arthritis (1985)
Eczema and Dermatitis (1985)
The Story Of Medicine (1985, 1998)
Natural Pain Control (1986)
Mindpower (1986)
Addicts and Addictions (1986)
Dr Vernon Coleman's Guide To Alternative Medicine (1988)
Stress Management Techniques (1988)
Overcoming Stress (1988)
Know Yourself (1988)
The Health Scandal (1988)
The 20 Minute Health Check (1989)
Sex For Everyone (1989)
Mind Over Body (1989)
Eat Green Lose Weight (1990)
Why Animal Experiments Must Stop (1991)
The Drugs Myth (1992)
How To Overcome Toxic Stress (1990)
Why Doctors Do More Harm Than Good (1993)
Stress and Relaxation (1993)

Complete Guide To Sex (1993)
How to Conquer Backache (1993)
How to Conquer Arthritis (1993)
Betrayal of Trust (1994)
Know Your Drugs (1994, 1997)
Food for Thought (1994, 2000)
The Traditional Home Doctor (1994)
I Hope Your Penis Shrivels Up (1994)
People Watching (1995)
Relief from IBS (1995)
The Parent's Handbook (1995)
Oral Sex: Bad Taste And Hard To Swallow? (1995)
Why Is Pubic Hair Curly? (1995)
Men in Dresses (1996)
Power over Cancer (1996)
Crossdressing (1996)
How to Conquer Arthritis (1996)
High Blood Pressure (1996)
How To Stop Your Doctor Killing You (1996)
Fighting For Animals (1996)
Alice and Other Friends (1996)
Spiritpower (1997)
Other People's Problems (1998)
How To Publish Your Own Book (1999)
How To Relax and Overcome Stress (1999)
Animal Rights – Human Wrongs (1999)
Superbody (1999)
The 101 Sexiest, Craziest, Most Outrageous Agony Column
        Questions (and Answers) of All Time (1999)
Strange But True (2000)
Daily Inspirations (2000)
Stomach Problems: Relief At Last (2001)
How To Overcome Guilt (2001)
How To Live Longer (2001)
Sex (2001)
How To Make Money While Watching TV (2001)
We Love Cats (2002)
England Our England (2002)
Rogue Nation (2003)

novels

The Village Cricket Tour (1990)
The Bilbury Chronicles (1992)
Bilbury Grange (1993)
Mrs Caldicot's Cabbage War (1993)
Bilbury Revels (1994)
Deadline (1994)
The Man Who Inherited a Golf Course (1995)
Bilbury Country (1996)
Second Innings (1999)
Around the Wicket (2000)
It's Never Too Late (2001)
Paris In My Springtime (2002)
Mrs Caldicot's Knickerbocker Glory (2003)

short stories

Bilbury Pie (1995)

on cricket

Thomas Winsden's Cricketing Almanack (1983)
Diary Of A Cricket Lover (1984)

as Edward Vernon

Practice Makes Perfect (1977)
Practise What You Preach (1978)
Getting Into Practice (1979)
Aphrodisiacs – An Owner's Manual (1983)
The Complete Guide To Life (1984)

as Marc Charbonnier

Tunnel (novel 1980)

with Alice

Alice's Diary (1989)
Alice's Adventures (1992)

with Dr Alan C Turin

No More Headaches (1981)

Rogue Nation

**Why America Is The Most
Dangerous State On Earth**

Vernon Coleman

Published by Blue Books, Publishing House, Trinity Place, Barnstaple, Devon EX32 9HJ, England.

ISBN: 1 899726 26 8

A catalogue record for this book is available from the British Library.

Printed by J.W. Arrowsmith Limited, Bristol

Dedication

To Donna Antoinette, who shares my concern and provides much valued love and much needed comfort in these deeply troubled times. These days we all need someone to hold our hand.

Preface

Rogue nation: 'a nation living apart from the rest, and of a savage or destructive disposition'

This is not an attack on the American people, except insofar as they have allowed a greedy and arrogant group of politicians and businessmen to hijack their country, and they have been too complacent and too lazy to question what they are told by probably the worst media in the world.

Sadly, most Americans still think they are living in a free country. Most of the rest of the world knows that they aren't. America is the real and present danger; a very real and very serious threat to world peace. America has the biggest stocks of weapons of mass destruction – and is the nation least likely to use those weapons responsibly. America is now the world's most dangerous enemy. America is a rogue nation, bullying its way into authority and power; unsettling other countries and constantly starting wars. America is responsible for worldwide economic and political chaos. Most Americans think they are fighting terrorists. Most of the rest of the world knows that Americans now are the terrorists. This book contains everything you need to know – and must know – about America.

Vernon Coleman, 2003

Introduction

For several days after the terrorist attacks on America in September 2001 I felt distinctly uneasy and strangely conflicted. I felt deeply sorry for the people who had lost their lives or been injured. I felt sad for their friends and relatives. Sympathy, pity, sadness – all the appropriate emotions were there. But there was something about the whole thing that made me feel uncomfortable. And I felt guilty but didn't know why.

It took me three days to work it out.

There are two distinct aspects to what happened in America in mid September 2001. First, and foremost, there was the human tragedy. Thousands of innocent people died suddenly. But, second, there was also the political aspect.

The day before the bombing I had prepared a first draft of an article pointing out that no nation (or group of nations) had ever had such good cause for declaring war on another nation as the rest of the world had for declaring war on the United States of America.

On the day of the bombing I thought it seemed inappropriate to make that point.

But there is no doubt that Americans have become enemies to much of the world – and are generally regarded with a mixture of fear and loathing. Americans have destroyed the global climate, caused irreparable harm to food supplies, sneered at freedom and democracy, bullied smaller countries and taken sides in disputes which did not concern them. There are bound to be many who feel aggrieved.

What happened in America on that September day merely confirmed the points I had planned to make.

In the days after the bombing we were repeatedly told that the attacks on the Pentagon (the symbol of American military might) and the World Trade Centre (the symbol of American imperialism and globalisation) were an attack on freedom and democracy.

To say that the attacks on America were an attack on freedom would have been laughable if the claim had not been made with apparent seriousness and in such sombre circumstances.

The attacks on America were attacks on America. They were, if anything, probably inspired by a yearning for freedom.

Have the Americans learnt absolutely nothing from the anti-globalisation campaigners and the protests at every meeting of world leaders?

America has done more to damage freedom than any other nation in history. America is the most imperialistic, colonial power since Rome. They have seized countries and bits of countries when it has suited them (ask the Spanish how the USA got hold of Florida, Cuba and the Philippines, ask the Mexicans how the USA acquired Texas and California and ask the French and the Native Americans how they view America's affection for other people's territory) and have interfered in the internal workings of countless nations around the world. They have helped to keep the civil war going in Ireland and they have caused chaos in Serbia and Kosovo.

The attacks on the USA were caused by a yearning for freedom. And the consequences of the attacks will be that all of us will have less freedom. To hear Bush and Blair talk about 'defending freedom' was nauseous, sanctimonious and hypocritical.

No rational, sensitive human being approves of violence, deaths, injury or suffering but the inescapable fact is that America, as a nation, has been responsible for more violence, more death, more injuries and more human suffering than any other modern nation. On the very day of the bombings in the USA the American Government indicated that it was 'unlikely' to prevent Sinn Fein from raising funds in the USA, even if it was shown that its allies in the IRA had been providing weapons training to anti-government Marxist guerrillas in Colombia.

Most people know that for years the IRA has received much of its funding from Americans. It has been American money which has been used to bomb Britons. And even in the aftermath of their own tragedy the Americans are still refusing to put a stop to that. Is that freedom? Or is it simply irresponsible and obscene? Surely, here is evidence that the difference between a terrorist and a freedom fighter is just a point of view? The Americans have threatened to punish any nation which harbours terrorists who attack the USA. By those standards the UK is entitled to attack America.

Let us offer Americans our sympathy, just as we offer it to Palestinians who have been dispossessed of their land, Indians who are starving because American companies have stolen their seeds, innocent Europeans who have been killed recently by American (and American inspired) bombing, and retreating Iraqis who were bombed by the American military.

But let us also do our best to teach Americans the real meaning of freedom and democracy.

For decades now America, long a reluctant ally (the Americans only entered the Second World War when they were forced to do so by Hitler declaring war on *them*) has been aggressive, abrasive and arrogant. The rest of the world has suffered at their hands for many years. The Americans have defended and cheered on Israeli atrocities and the contemptuous American government has initiated and sustained military action throughout the world in order to keep its own armaments industry happy. The attack on America was a grotesque crime. But the savage activities of the Israelis have for years been an equal disgrace. And yet the Americans have supported those attacks.

How wonderful it would be if America could have learnt a little, and maybe grown in wisdom and stature, from what happened on September 11th. How wonderful it would be if the permanent memorial to the lives which were lost could be a more understanding, peaceful, sensitive America.

Some hope.

USA president George W. Bush behaved appallingly during the crisis. Bush is not a natural leader. He seems rather dim-witted and is no statesman. He scuttled off and hid at the first sign of trouble. A real leader would have visited the damaged areas and shown himself to his people. The photographs showed a man apparently tormented by a great sense of his own personal inadequacy.

Immediately after September 11th I wrote that: 'having shown himself to be a coward, Bush will probably try to prove himself a bully. He seems certain to pick a fight with all those parts of the world which do not approve of America.'

Fighting those parts of the world which don't like America is going to be a big fight. It's a fight which America cannot win. (You would think that America would know, by now, that you can't win wars against passionate guerrillas and terrorists. They seem to have forgotten Korea and Vietnam.) And it is a fight which will almost certainly lead to more deaths (including the great unacceptable – the deaths of American servicemen).

If Bush picks a war against everyone who dislikes America he will find himself building up yet more resentment against the world's richest and most powerful country.

The world's sympathy went out to America. On a human level that was right, proper and appropriate. But America also expected, demanded – and received – political sympathy. And that was wrong, improper and inappropriate.

Bush wants to spend $500 billion on his new national missile defence system. It won't provide a 100 per cent defence against a ballistic missile attack. And it won't provide any sort of defence against terrorists. He would gain friends around the world if he spent that money trying to put right some of the damage done to the rest of the world by American corporations during the last few decades. It was, after all, those selfish corporate policies which helped build America's wealth.

Bush has described his coming 'war against terrorism' as a fight between good and evil. What he has to understand is that to most of the world he himself represents the greatest of all modern evils.

The wicked attack on America was a massive tragedy; a cause of great sadness to everyone. But in the long run it will help no one if we allow our personal feelings of sorrow for those who died or were injured to alter our feelings about the political and economic activities of the United States of America.

Vernon Coleman, 2003

1

'This is the man who tried to kill my daddy.'
GEORGE W. BUSH, ALLEGEDLY THE WORLD'S MOST POWERFUL
MAN, EXPLAINING WHY THE WORLD SHOULD GO TO WAR AGAINST IRAQ
AND TOPPLE SADDAM HUSSEIN.

2

America executes children and the mentally retarded. Only six countries impose the death penalty on children. They are: Iran, Nigeria, Pakistan, Saudi Arabia, Yemen and the United States of America.

3

America only entered World War I (on the side of Britain and France) after both its new allies and new enemies were pretty much exhausted by the fighting. Once it agreed to join in the war America imposed conditions which included the demand that America's economic and political objectives be taken into account when the war was over. One of those objectives was access to new sources of raw materials, particularly oil. In February 1919, Sit Arthur Hirtzel, a leading British official warned: 'It should be borne in mind that the Standard Oil Company is very anxious to take over Iraq.'

America demanded that its oil companies be allowed to negotiate freely with the new puppet monarchy of King Faisal (the monarch whom the British had put on the throne in Iraq). And so Iraq's oil was divided up between the allies. Five per cent of the oil went to an oil magnate called Gulbenkian (known as 'Mr Five Per Cent' who had helped negotiate the agreement). The other 95 per cent was split four ways between Britain, France, Holland and the United States of America. Companies now known as British Petroleum, Shell, Mobil and Exxon pretty much had a monopoly of the oil available. (Iraqi oil was split this way until 1958 when there was a revolution in Iraq.)

American influence in the region was sealed when the al-Saud family and the United States of America created Saudi Arabia in the 1930s, pretty much as an American colony. It was no coincidence that the American Embassy in Riyadh, the capital city, was situated in the local oil company building.

The Americans were not, however, satisfied with their share of Middle East oil. They wanted control. They had to get rid of the British. And their chance came with the Second World War.

The Americans unceasingly portray themselves as Britain's saviour. This is a wicked misrepresentation. As it had been in the Great War, America was ruthlessly opportunistic.

Britain was greatly weakened by the Second World War but America grew tremendously in power as a result of what happened in the early 1940s. The Roosevelt and Truman administrations (which were dominated by banking and oil interests) decided to restructure the world to ensure that the USA would be on top. They wanted control of the world's oil. They wanted USA dominated globalisation (to which end they created the International Monetary Fund and the World Bank in 1944). They wanted the dollar to be the only significant world currency. And they wanted the USA to have military superiority in all types of weapons.

Winston Churchill was so worried by what he could see happening that on March 4th 1944 (three months before the D Day invasion of Normandy) he sought assurance from the USA that she would not try to take over British oil interests.

He wrote to USA president Roosevelt saying: 'Thank you very much for your assurances about no sheep's eyes on our oilfields in Iran and Iraq. Let me reciprocate by giving you the fullest assurance that we have no thought of trying to horn in upon your interests or property in Saudi Arabia. My position in this, as in all matters, is that Great Britain seeks no advantage, territorial or otherwise, as a result of this war. On the other hand, she will not be deprived of anything which rightly belongs to her after having given her best services to the good cause, at least not so long as your humble servant is entrusted with the conduct of affairs.'

Sadly, there was nothing that even Churchill could do to save Britain from its new 'enemy'. In 1953, a CIA coup which put the Shah in power gave Iran to the United States of America. (The Americans also helped the Shah form his much hated secret police.)

And within a couple of years after that Iraq was jointly controlled by America and Britain.

In 1955 America set up the Baghdad Pact, which was designed, at least in part, to oppose the rise of Arab liberation movements in the Middle East. Britain and Iraq were signatories, although Iraq was independent only in name. The British still had military airfields in Iraq which was ruled by a corrupt monarchy. The people of Iraq, despite having a huge quantity of the world's oil under their feet, were still starving and living in abject poverty.

Things changed in Iraq in 1958. A military rebellion launched a revolution which was to have dramatic consequences on the world. The day after the revolution started the Americans put 20,000 marines into Lebanon and over 6,000 British paratroopers dropped into Jordan. Under Eisenhower's leadership the USA and the UK had made it clear that they would go to war to protect their interests in Lebanon and Jordan.

The British, rather naively, thought that they were simply protecting their interests outside Iraq. The Americans had bigger thoughts. They wanted to go into Iraq, overturn the revolution and put a new puppet government (friendly to the USA, of course) in charge in Baghdad.

But the Americans were stopped. The Iraq revolution was too big. And it had too much support from other Arab countries, from the People's Republic of China and from the USSR. The Americans glumly gave up their imperialist plans.

But they didn't give up completely.

The thwarted Americans added Iraq to their growing list of terrorist nations and gave great support to right wing Kurdish elements who were fighting the Iraqi Government. Then, in the late 1970s the Americans supported the government of Saddam Hussein in its fight against communism. In the 1980s the Americans supported (with money and arms) Saddam Hussein's Iraq in its eight year war against Iran, a country over which America had lost control during Iran's Islamic Revolution of 1979. The Americans openly admitted that they were intervening in order to safeguard their access to the region's oil and they slightly less openly hoped that Iraq and Iran would weaken one another and enable the USA to take over. 'I hope they kill each other,' former Secretary of State Henry Kissinger is said to have remarked. The Americans provided Iraq's air force with satellite photographs of Iranian targets and sent anti-aircraft missiles to Iran so that the Iranians could shoot down the aircraft which the Iraqis sent over. America fought on both sides in this war and was well aware that Saddam Hussein was using chemical weapons. Over a million people died and both countries were left much weaker. (Bizarrely, and hypocritically, in 2003 George W. Bush was claiming that Saddam Hussein's use of chemical weapons in this war was one of the main reasons for attacking Iraq.) The money America made from selling missiles to Iran was used to finance the Contras who were fighting the socialist government in Nicaragua. Reagan, USA President at the time, disapproved of socialist regimes and wanted to get rid of this one in particular. (It is perhaps unfair to ascribe such depth of feeling to Reagan himself, rather than to his advisors.)

The war between Iraq and Iran didn't finish until 1988, by which time Iraq had become friendly with the USSR.

But then the USSR was taken over by Gorbachev, who wanted an end to the cold war and a permanent detente with America. Gorbachev withdrew Soviet support from Iraq (as he had withdrawn it from countries in Eastern Europe) and the world suddenly changed yet again.

After the war with Iran Saddam Hussein had accumulated massive debts. The low price of oil meant that his income didn't match his national outgoings. The Iraqi president accused Kuwait of drilling for oil in Iraqi territory and then announced that Kuwait wasn't a separate nation at all but was a province of Iraq. Iraqi troops invaded Kuwait in 1990. America (with an international force) attacked, the resultant war was over in weeks and in 1991 the Americans got back into Iraq. In the decade that followed they have used sanctions, bombings and blockades to weaken the Iraqi people and to destroy their spirit. American sanctions against Iraq do not target Saddam Hussein, they target the Iraqi people.

Now the Americans, led by oil man George W. Bush are going back into Iraq. The Americans do not give a fig for human rights and they know that Saddam Hussein is no threat to America. They know well that he has no weapons of mass destruction. (And even if he did have them the Americans have the military capability to destroy Iraq in seconds.) They surely also know that Saddam Hussein has nothing in common with Osama bin Laden.

America is going back into Iraq for the same, good old reason. Oil.

4

'I am willing to love all mankind, except an American.'
SAMUEL JOHNSON

5

The USA is the meanest country in the world – 22nd out of 22 – when it comes to foreign aid. Denmark gives 1.01 per cent of its GDP to foreign aid. America gives 0.1 per cent – and most of that goes to Israel for arms purchases (from American arms companies). America's foreign aid is organised in such a way that the only country which really benefits is America.

6

Since the gold standard was abandoned the USA has benefited from having the world's major 'base' currency. The USA gets free money from the rest of the world because it can issue dollars to be used as cash in other countries. America is successful because it made the money rules to suit itself – and the rest of the world has to live (or die) by those rules. At the end of World War II (and the real beginning of America's modern prosperity) the USA devised the Bretton Woods Agreement which gave the USA the right to have its dollars considered the same as gold in Central Banks throughout the world. In 1971 president Nixon refused to continue exchanging dollars for gold. At this point America gave itself the right to print as much money as it wanted. For the last thirty years the Americans have had the right to create their own wealth – at the expense of the rest of the world. The world is controlled by American currency policy. This is what has given Americans the wealth and power which they believe makes them superior to the rest of the world.

The Americans have bought companies, land and so on and paid for everything in dollars – which their Government had printed. Every year for a decade now around $400 billion has left the USA and been used to buy property in other countries. America has, inevitably, got richer and richer. And the rest of the world has got poorer and poorer. This is a sort of American tax on everyone else. The Americans have no intention of ever bringing those dollars back to their shore. And they have no intention of replacing the dollars with real goods and services. Other countries have to 'buy' imports by exporting goods or services. This is not true for America. America's annual trade deficit is simply a massive tax on the rest of the world. America has 'stolen' the world and has left other countries impoverished as a result. America cannot lose. Every other country has already lost because for decades America has been buying 'things' without paying for them.

7

Did the CIA know about the attacks on New York and Washington? Did Bush? I don't know. But I wouldn't rule it out. Too ruthless? Hardly. It is, after all, the American Government which encourage companies to manufacture land mines which are specifically designed to be triggered by young children – not to kill them but just to blow off a leg or a foot. (The rationale being that this puts pressure on the local health services and that the sight of lots of limbless children hobbling around demoralises the affected population.)

It was America which used napalm with such enthusiasm when interfering in Vietnam.

This is the Government which insists on vaccinating children – even though they must know that vaccines are often neither safe nor effective.

This is the Government which subsidises the growing of tobacco, which protects tobacco company advertising and which makes vast profits out of the sale of tobacco products.

This is the Government which defends companies which force genetically engineered products on an unwilling population, and which does nothing to preserve the environment (even though it knows that these policies are directly responsible for such dramatic changes in the weather that flooding has become a serious problem in large areas of the world).

America has ruthlessly pursued policies which have resulted in vast numbers of deaths. Are American leaders and policy makers ruthless enough to regard the death of a few thousand civilians a fair exchange for an end to anti-globalisation protests and an opportunity to introduce new legislation controlling the privacy and freedom of ordinary citizens?

Even much loved British bulldog Winston Churchill sacrificed Coventry during the Second World War so that the Germans wouldn't know that the British could decode their communications.

8

Within months of the September 11th attack on New York, the Americans had (with Britain's help) started a revenge war against Afghanistan which was accused of harbouring the man who was accused of masterminding the attack.

9

Why not try Osama bin Laden in his absence. Then, if he is found guilty, he can be sought and arrested in the normal manner. Isn't that the proper way to go about things?

10

The Americans often claim that they entered the Second World War after the Japanese attacked Pearl Harbour but this is not entirely true. It is a popular misconception that America declared war on Germany. In fact it was the other way round. The Americans only came into World War II because Germany declared war on them. Churchill was delighted because he had, of course, spent a considerable amount of time unsuccessfully trying to persuade the Americans to take part in the war.

11

Pushed to explain why we should start a war on Iraq (and doubtless kill thousands of innocent citizens) USA and UK Government hawks claimed that if someone gave Iraq the essential materials they might be able to make a nuclear bomb within a year. This is rather like the police saying that they decided to shoot a man because they were worried that if someone gave him a gun he might use it. America's belligerence and warmongering is by far the greatest threat to world peace. None of Iraq's neighbouring countries felt threatened by Iraq – indeed they were opposed to a war. No direct threat to Britain, Europe or America has ever been demonstrated.

12

By the middle of January 2002 the Bush 'n' Blair alliance had dropped £1.4 billion worth of bombs on Afghanistan and had killed over 4,000 civilians. At that point the number of innocents killed in Afghanistan in this most obscene example of 'an eye for an eye' justice considerably exceeded the number killed in America on September 11th.

13

America describes itself as the 'Land of the Free' but that really is something of a joke. America is one of the most repressed nations on the planet. The police and various government agencies have an enormous amount of power. To say that America is a fascist state is as much of an understatement as it is a joke to say that it is the land of the free.

Is America the land of the free if you happen to have been born on an Indian reservation? Is it the land of the free for blacks? American authorities have absurd amounts of power over their citizens. (Just ask those Americans who have been wrongly killed, assaulted or arrested by gun waving police or drug enforcement officials what they think of freedom).

As numerous presidents and high ranking officials have shown, most Americans have no idea where other countries are – or what their political affiliations might be. America has more muggings than any other country on earth. Thanks to absurdly lenient gun laws visitors are more likely to be shot and killed in America than in any other so-called civilised country. America is home to evangelical Christian fundamentalists and has made corruption among politicians acceptable. America has more high tech hospitals than anywhere else on earth. But has one of the lowest life expectation rates in the developed world. Astonishingly, there is more social stratification in the USA (much of it racial) than there is in Britain. America lacks culture and their comedy is often childishly unsophisticated. It is, in short, a nation of children trying to be worldly.

14

'Why do so many people hate the United States so much? One common answer is that it does hateful things. America is the world's biggest polluter, it refuses to curb greenhouse emissions, monopolises wealth and does nothing to help poor countries; it insists on free trade for the benefit of its corporations, it supports Israeli oppression of Palestinians, humiliates Muslims and generally wields its cultural, economic and military might with wanton arrogance.'
HENRI ASTIER, THE BUSINESS NEWSPAPER, 26.1.2003

15

If you exclude the Native Americans, the United States of America is populated exclusively by illegal aliens.

16

'The inhabitants of Greece are the Greecians.'
GEORGE W. BUSH, ALLEGEDLY THE WORLD'S MOST POWERFUL MAN.

17

American-owned multinational corporations employ child labour in order to keep their prices down.

18

'Americans believe that everything can be solved by violence. Locally they deal with problems by shooting one another. Internationally they deal with problems by starting wars.'
READER'S LETTER

19

The average American uses the car for 93 per cent of all trips outside the home. Including the yardage covered pushing a supermarket trolley, and the distance covered from front door to car and back again, the average American walks no more than 350 yards a day. This could, perhaps, help explain why obesity is endemic in the USA.

One in two Americans are seriously overweight and at least a third of adults in the USA are clinically obese. That doesn't mean just overweight or plump. It means grossly, offensively, disgustingly fat. Obese individuals are far more likely to suffer from just about every disease imaginable.

The obesity of Americans has, I fear, become something of an international joke. In France recently I got into a lift which carried a notice informing passengers that the lift's capacity was 'Eight persons or two Americans'.

20

The Americans become very upset when innocent American citizens are killed by military or terrorist action. And yet it was the Americans who invented the phrase 'collateral damage' to describe the deaths of civilians. Along with the phrase, the Americans invented the immoral and elitist philosophy that it doesn't matter a damn if civilians die as long as they aren't American.

21

Every year over one million Americans declare bankruptcy. That's an awful lot of personal misery for a supposedly rich country.

22

The hypocrisy of the George W. Bush and Tony Blair alliance continues to startle even experienced commentators. The Americans (aided and abetted by the British) bombed the life out of the remaining, innocent and now invariably homeless Afghans in a futile search for a man they thought might have been responsible for the attack on America. But, at the same time, both Bush and Blair continue to suck up to the IRA.

The Americans have for years been responsible for funding the IRA – and still they refuse to stop. Blair's Government bends over backwards to appease and please IRA leaders because Blair wants to convince the world that he has solved the 'Irish problem'. Even he presumably finds it a little difficult to act the part of a 'world leader' when he still has a civil war going on at home.

23

It seems that the $7 million support the tobacco industry gave to George W. Bush's presidential campaign produced a good harvest. Shortly after Bush's election it was clear that tobacco companies would save an estimated $100 billion when a proposed federal lawsuit was dropped. Not a bad rate of return.

On a similar note, the oil companies which backed Bush financially were said to be pleased at his dumping of the Kyoto protocol.

24

'There ought to be limits to freedom.'
GEORGE W. BUSH, PRESIDENT OF THE USA

25

It has been widely rumoured that the Americans knew about the attacks which so affected America on September 11th 2001 but did nothing to stop them. The attacks were, so the rumour goes, perceived as 'too convenient to the establishment' to stop.

One rumour, circulating within hours on September 11th, was that the attack would be used to excuse a global war to replace the failing drugs war, to bring an end to anti-American campaigns in the West, to stop anti-globalisation campaigners protesting at G7 meetings and to enable the American and British governments to introduce tougher new security, new banking laws and new ID rules.

The drugs war had been used by the Americans and others to bring in a whole raft of invasive laws. By using the drugs war as an excuse politicians and police had been able to get rid of many of the public's traditional freedoms. But, as an excuse, the drugs war was beginning to pall. Most people had recognised that we would all be better off if drugs were simply decriminalised.

So, how convenient it was that the Americans had found itself an excuse for a never-ending war against terrorism – a new war that would provide an excuse for many new losses of freedom.

Naturally, political leaders dismiss such rumours as the 'ravings of unhinged minds' and the result of 'paranoia'.

But, they would, wouldn't they?

26

'The Americans are bombing Iraq because they want their oil, because Bush senior is still embarrassed about the last fiasco and because the Americans want to please the Israelis. I do wish they would be honest about it.'
LETTER FROM 86-YEAR-OLD SOLDIER.

27

A survey found that a large number of science textbooks used in the USA are riddled with errors.

28

During the build-up to the war on Iraq, American president George W. Bush wasn't too busy to do a bit of fund raising. For example, he spoke at one dinner where guests were charged $250 a head. Guests who wanted to have their photo taken with Mr Bush had to pay an extra $4,000. According to the Financial Times Mr Bush has now raised more than £73 million in this way.

29

The Americans now spend more on fast food than they spend on higher education, new cars, personal computers or computer software. In the year 2000 Americans spent more than $110 billion on burgers, chips and other fast food delicacies. An estimated one out of every eight workers in the USA has at one point been employed by one chain alone – which also happens to be the largest owner of retail property in the world. And the fast food industry is arguably America's most successful global export.

Has all this been for good or bad? There is no doubt that the burger chains' demands have encouraged fundamental changes in the way that cattle are raised, slaughtered and processed. The constant search for lower prices means that meat-packing has become an extremely dangerous job. Low and insanitary standards are reported to have led to many workers being injured and to the introduction of dangerous bacteria – such as various hazardous strains of e.coli.

It is now claimed that 200,000 Americans get food poisoning daily. Modern processed meats are said to leave more faecal bacteria in the average American kitchen sink than can be found on the average American toilet seat.

And the food sold in the fast food chains doesn't bear much resemblance to real food since the flavours and textures are chemically produced.

30

I meet a good many people from different countries and in my experience the relatively small number of Americans who do venture outside their own country tend to wander around the world in a cocoon of Americanism. They prefer to stay at American chain hotels. They mix with Americans. They rarely speak any foreign languages and they read only American newspapers and magazines. They have a tendency to treat non-Americans as second class citizens. It is hardly surprising that Americans, as a whole, show very little understanding of the needs and wants of the citizens of other countries.

31

It is generally accepted that one of the reasons why the Americans are so desperate to grab Iraq's oil is that they are worried about the instability in Saudi Arabia. It is agreed by commentators that it is only a matter of time before there is some sort of revolution in Saudi Arabia. Most Middle Eastern oil comes from Iran, Iraq or

Saudi Arabia, or from countries such as Kuwait which are vulnerable to instability in those countries.

32

America can never win against terrorists because there are more terrorists prepared to die for what they believe than there are Americans prepared to die for what they believe.

33

The Americans always claim that their's is the 'land of the free' and that their repressive, isolationist laws are designed to protect freedom. There are those who might disagree. For example, consider the young American with paedophile tendencies who wrote down some of his fictitious fantasies for his own entertainment. I have no sympathy for paedophiles. Those who abuse children need to be locked away in a very safe place. But when this young man's parents found their son's journal they handed it over to the police hoping that he would be offered treatment. Instead, the young man was charged with 'pandering obscenity', found guilty and sentenced to seven years in prison. The prosecutor claimed that even though the man had not passed on his secret thoughts to anyone else he had committed a felony.

34

'There isn't much demand for the sort of work older people can do.'
A twenty-something American Human Resources director

35

According to American Justice Department, on any given day two million American children have a parent or close relative in prison.

Five million more have parents who have been in prison at some time in the past.

36

Most of the terrorists who attacked America on September 11th came from Saudi Arabia. The Americans did not, however, ever contemplate starting a war against Saudi Arabia.

37

The war in Afghanistan cost Britain twice what it spends annually on cancer treatment. There was never any cogent reason given for Britain to declare war on Afghanistan. Bizarrely, Britons and Americans were told that they were fighting for freedom and democracy.

38

Following America's example, the Defence Secretary in the UK claimed that Britain's Armed Forces are to be reshaped because their future role will be to invade 'failed states'.

Who is going to decide which states have failed and need to be invaded? What criteria will be used? These questions have, apparently, never been asked, let alone answered.

39

'Saddam is a constant irritant to the Bush family because he has lasted through eight years of Clinton and now into another Bush generation.'
READER'S LETTER

40

'I am for peace. By killing innocent people in a war we will achieve nothing.
The statement of George W. Bush that 'either you are with America or you
are with the terrorists' is disgraceful and nothing short of a nasty threat, as
many people are neither with America or the terrorists. There were indeed
thousands of innocent lives taken in the New York carnage, however America
has also taken the lives of far more equally innocent people. Are they not every
bit as important? Apparently not because they were not American. America
interferes in too many countries. I believe that the USA Government is mainly
responsible for creating Islamic terrorism. Nothing will ever be gained from
the evil legalised destruction of innocent lives.'
READER'S LETTER

41

According to the Journal of the American Medical Association the
overall incidence of serious Adverse Drug Reactions in America is
now 6.7 per cent, while the incidence of fatal Adverse Drug Reactions is 0.32 per cent of hospitalised patients. JAMA estimates that
in one year well over two million hospitalised patients in the USA
have serious Adverse Drug Reactions while 106,000 have fatal
Adverse Drug Reactions (this means that they die).

According to JAMA these figures mean that Adverse Drug Reactions are now between the fourth and sixth leading cause of death
in the USA.

In compiling this data JAMA excluded errors in drug administration, noncompliance, overdose, drug abuse, therapeutic failures
and possible Adverse Drug Reactions. Serious Adverse Drug Reactions were defined as those which required treatment in hospital,
were permanently disabling or resulted in death.

42

'The inept Americans had to beg Britain for help in Afghanistan recently.
'We don't do mountains,' one dispirited American soldier is said to have

commented. What a pity the Americans didn't realise that Afghanistan is a rather hilly country before they decided to wage unofficial war on it. Another officer told his men not to wander off the metalled roads because of the risk of land mines. Did the Americans seriously expect bin Laden and his colleagues to sit patiently on a metalled road, waiting to be caught?'
READER'S LETTER

43

'When tragedies occur in the 'rest of the world' (such as floods in Pakistan and India or monsoons in S.E. Asia) American television devotes about 90 seconds to it, even though thousands may die. A tragedy in which hundreds die is breaking news in the USA for one day only because only American lives matter. An earthquake in Italy, which killed numerous schoolchildren, was given the usual 90 seconds on American television but a sniper who killed only 12 received saturation TV coverage 24 hours a day for three weeks. When the USA pays out money to victims of air crashes Americans get more money than non American citizens. Obviously American lives are more valuable than others.'
CHEVALIER HARRY D SCHULTZ, AUTHOR AND PUBLISHER OF *HSL NEWSLETTER.* (WWW.HSLETTER.COM.)

44

The Labour Government in the UK sold its official Ministry of Defence research laboratories to an American organisation called the Carlyle Group. The Carlyle Group has close and powerful connections with the USA Government – particularly the Bush bit.

45

'All this talk about Iraq having chemical weapons is no longer valid.'
SCOTT RITTER, FORMER UN WEAPONS INSPECTOR

46

Americans commonly claim that they invented the motor-car, the telephone, the television and the internet. In fact these are just a few of many inventions which originated in Europe but were subsequently exploited (most profitably) by Americans.

47

You cannot destroy terrorism unless you also destroy freedom.

48

The Americans have announced that they intend to impose democracy on Iraq. They have not yet explained precisely how one nation (an aggressor) can impose democracy on another. (And shouldn't America try installing democracy at home before they attempt to impose it on another country?)

49

'The UN,' said George W. Bush in February 2003, as he waited for the UN security council to decide whether or not to sanction a war against Iraq, 'gets to decide whether it is going to be relevant.' (Bush presumably believes that if the UN doesn't agree with the USA it is irrelevant.)

50

'The French don't have a word for 'entrepreneur'.'
GEORGE W. BUSH, PRESIDENT OF THE USA, OBVIOUSLY NOT
REALISING THAT THE WORD 'ENTREPRENEUR' IS A FRENCH WORD.

51

The American House of Representatives voted against a proposal to curb sales and rentals of graphically violent films to children. It was presumably thought that such a curb would adversely affect the profits of those making and renting out such films.

52

'Americans worry a great deal about the import of cocaine and other drugs into the USA, but little is done to halt the far more deadly export of tobacco into the nations of the Third World.'
ROBERT N. PROCTOR

53

'Is the USA ready for self-government?'
SCRAWLED ON A WALL IN NEW YORK.

54

The USA uses more of the world's resources than the rest of the world put together.

55

During his presidential campaign genius George W. Bush had to be told the meaning of the word 'vegan' by an aide.

56

In late February 2003, as America prepared to start a war against Iraq, the USA had armed forces in Oman, Yemen, Turkey, Saudi

Arabia, Bosnia, Kosovo, Argentine, Brazil, Paraguay, Colombia, Philippines, Georgia, Djibouti and Afghanistan. In nations where American soldiers weren't actually killing the natives themselves they were training local government forces to kill alleged terrorists or guerillas threatening oil pipelines.

57

One of the last things vice president Al Gore did, before sending away his lawyers and joining the political unemployment line, was to set up, with America's Environmental Protection Agency (EPA) something called the Child Health Testing Program.

The American government decided not to bother actually testing air, water or food to find out which chemicals were around in the greatest abundance – and which, therefore, might be causing the most problems.

They decided not to bother warning parents against which foods contained dangerous chemicals.

They decided not to slap any controls on the way chemicals are used.

They decided not to do proper laboratory tests which would identify the most dangerous chemicals.

Instead, they chose to set up a huge animal testing programme – apparently believing that this would help them find out exactly what chemicals are toxic and what dosages are safe for children.

It is difficult to define precisely how stupid this programme is. By comparison, Napoleon's decision to lay siege to Moscow was a military masterstroke. The Japanese decision to bomb Pearl Harbour was an exhibition of strategic genius. And the decision to send American troops to South Vietnam was politically brilliant.

America's plan is a simple one.

If chemical A doesn't kill rats (or make them obviously ill) then it will be deemed safe to put into baby food.

If chemical B only kills rats in large doses, then small doses will be considered safe for babies and children.

This is the biggest craziest, most obscene, most utterly pointless testing programme in history.

It is pointless because rats, mice, rabbits, cats, dogs and so on are all different to one another. And they are certainly, unquestion-ably different to human beings. The evidence clearly shows that tests done on animals are misleading and cannot be applied to hu-man beings. (See my books *Betrayal of Trust, Animal Rights Human Wrongs, Why Animal Experiments Must Stop* etc. for the evidence.)

58

'George thinks a bibliography is the story of the guys who wrote the Bible.'
MRS GEORGE W. BUSH, TALKING ABOUT HER HUSBAND.

59

The Americans gave us hamburgers and turned the concept of 'fast food' into the reality of 'junk food'. They gave us MTV twenty-second-television. And they force fed us genetically engineered food. As long ago as 1999 nearly half of the soybeans and well over a third of the corn grown in the USA were genetically modified. Gene spliced plants are now grown on 30 million hectares of USA farmland. Despite well founded fear and a natural sense of scepti-cism from the rest of the world, some big food companies outside the USA now say that because of the Americans they can't guaran-tee that their products are free of genetically engineered foods.

To all this we must add the fact that the Americans destroyed the English language and our morals by inventing such horrendous phrases as: 'killed by friendly fire'.

And these people are supposed to be Britain's allies?

60

In 2002, American generals persuaded George W. Bush, USA presi-dent, not to destroy America's stocks of smallpox virus. Why does America need a large stock of smallpox virus?

61

British Premier Tony Blair claims that America and the UK can, if they work together, solve all the world's problems. This is the politician under whose government Britain has acquired the highest crime rate in the developed world, the worst health care service, the worst transport system and the fastest rising taxes. This is the same Tony Blair who stayed in the House of Commons for just 35 minutes when his fellow MPs spent hours debating whether Britain should, or should not, join the Americans in waging war on Iraq. (He left the most important debate the House of Commons had had for decades because he had a television engagement.)

The number of Britons who have fled Britain and sought refuge in France and Spain now exceeds the number of Iraqis who have fled Saddam Hussein's regime in Iraq.

62

USA president George W. Bush and UK prime minister Tony Blair compared those who opposed the 2003 war against Iraq with those who sought peace with Hitler in the 1930s. But if we must compare any modern political leader to 1930s Hitler then we must pick George W. Bush. It is Bush, not Hussein, who is threatening world peace. It is Bush, not Hussein, who is itching to use his weapons of mass destruction.

63

Britain's role in supporting America's war against Afghanistan was compared by eminent historian Corelli Barnett, to that of the bucket and shovel men who follow the procession at the Lord Mayor's Show in London.

64

'American politicians are forced to support Israel because of the power the Jewish community has in the USA. It is the American support for a country which illegally occupies Arab land, and which ruthlessly and cruelly suppresses the Palestinian people, which is at the heart of the world's problems.'
READER'S LETTER

65

'I think that if you know what you believe, it makes it a lot easier to answer questions. I can't answer your question.'
GEORGE W. BUSH, PRESIDENT OF THE USA, IN A MOMENT OF PAINFUL AND REVEALING HONESTY.

66

The Americans claim the world envies them because they are rich. But are they? The average American family works for fifty years and at the end of that time will have managed to amass savings of just £1,400.

Some 60 million Americans live at or below the official poverty line and 45 million are in temporary or part-time jobs which carry no benefits or security.

67

It is a classic American ploy to make something happen, or to pretend something has happened, so they have an excuse to do what they wanted to do in the first place – usually something aggressive and often something indefensible. (See also entry 382.)

The American Government desperately wanted an excuse to clamp down on demonstrations against globalism and capitalism. I believe that even if the atrocities of September 11th were not planned by members of the American ruling establishment, they were authorised by establishment figures. I know that this sounds shocking but that doesn't make it impossible.

Led by America, governments around the world have been amazingly quick to introduce new legislation. Nearly all of this new legislation just happened to be prepared and ready to turn into laws. Most of this legislation is allegedly being introduced to control terrorism.

You don't need to be very bright to realise that the legislation will have a minimal impact on terrorists but a massive impact on ordinary citizens.

68

In one recent twelve month period, Catholic hospitals in a single American city refused to offer morning-after pills to more than 1,000 rape victims. Some civilisation.

69

An American company has spent the last 30 years collecting information. It now has dossiers on 160 million Americans and its database includes 20 million unlisted telephone numbers. How does it get them? Mostly from the warranty cards innocent and trusting people fill in when they buy electrical appliances. The company sells the information – including the unlisted telephone numbers – to law enforcement agencies, private investigators, lawyers and debt collectors. Because it combines public record information with consumer information purchased from the private sector, this company is said to be better at finding people than the police are. However, it isn't just debt collectors and lawyers who buy this sort of information. Companies buy it so that they can judge the quality of new customers. Large companies use 'caller ID' to identify callers by their phone number. The company employee taking the call can click into software which gives him an enormous amount of information about you, your purchasing power, your credit cards, your employment, your size and shape and your likes and dislikes.

Within seconds that stranger will know as much (or more) about the American caller as the caller's friends and relatives.

Courtesy of the USA, this system will soon be available throughout the rest of the world.

70

The war on terrorism is in reality a war on freedom, enabling politicians to suppress dissidents and political opponents.

71

Most publishers and broadcasters are terrified to criticise the Americans because of the risk of economic reprisals.

72

The way the Americans are treating their prisoners in their illegal concentration camp at Guantanamo Bay is a disgrace. The Pentagon claims that the men being kept there are 'unlawful combatants'. But what does that mean? There is no such category in international law. People who are detained are either criminals (in which case they should be charged and processed through the normal legal process) or else they are prisoners of war protected by the Geneva Conventions. The Americans have devised a third definition simply to assuage their own yearning for revenge and once again they have proved themselves to be extraordinarily hypocritical.

Either America is at war with Afghanistan or it isn't. If it is then the prisoners they capture must be prisoners of war. If it isn't then why the hell have they bombed the place to bits? (I seem to remember that Bush defined it as a war very early and excused the bombing of civilians in Afghanistan by claiming that it was a 'war on terrorism'.) America seems to change the rules whenever it suits them. Amazingly, they do not realise that the way they treat their prisoners will have an enormous influence on the way America is viewed by Muslims everywhere.

Incidentally, in the late 1990s, an American citizen was tried by a military court in Peru on the charge that she was a member of a terrorist group. The American Government complained that the trial did not satisfy the requirements of due process and that proceedings in Peru's military courts did not meet internationally accepted standards of openness, fairness and due process.

The Americans really can't have it both ways. The real tragedy of America's childish and rather crude yearning for revenge is that dictators everywhere will now believe that they too can ignore the Geneva Convention with impunity.

Once again America, exhibiting breathtaking arrogance, has damaged human rights and freedoms.

73

While trying to persuade the world to accept their plan to declare war on Iraq (so that they could grab the oil) the American government claimed that Iraq had weapons of mass destruction. They boasted that they had 'undeniable' evidence proving that Saddam Hussein was double dealing over disarmament. This turned out to be a massive lie. United Nations inspectors later described American intelligence on Iraq's alleged weapons of mass destruction as 'garbage'. The United Nations weapons team said that they had found nothing at an alleged nuclear research site shown in satellite pictures by the Americans. The United Nations weapons inspectors reported that other claims (made by the Americans) relating to nuclear research and missiles were also fake.

74

At the time when the Americans and British were planning to wage war on Iraq over 50 per cent of the population of Iraq was under the age of 15. (Millions of adults had already been killed by American bombing raids and by illness caused by the fact that the Americans refused to allow the Iraqis to have clean drinking water.)

75

The Americans did nothing to support Britain during the Blitz in World War II. They were waiting to see if they would lose before deciding which side to support. It was only when the Germans declared war on them that the Americans became unwillingly involved in the Second World War. Those who claim differently are distorting history to serve their own ends.

I can understand Americans wanting to hide the truth but I am appalled that British politicians deliberately falsify the facts.

76

'My ex-daughter-in-law whispered to me that the brother of my granddaughter's favourite baby sitter was among the missing.'
WRITER EXPLAINING IN AMERICAN MAGAZINE *VANITY FAIR* HOW HE HAD BEEN PERSONALLY AFFECTED BY THE ATTACK OF 11TH SEPTEMBER 2001.

77

'American owned news programmes and newspapers are constantly full of misinformation. We can't trust the mass media — they print what they are told, and are clearly too scared to question anything serious or to provide truly questioning, independent criticism on any matter of current affairs.'
READER'S LETTER

78

There is one question which should be asked (but rarely is).

Who stands to gain most — and in what ways — if the West wages a war on Muslims?

79

Back in the late 1980s and early 1990s, I worked out that the British Government's bizarrely irresponsible AIDS campaign had been responsible for more deaths than AIDS itself; largely because numerous people, consumed by anxiety, had killed themselves.

More recently, the American Government has deliberately spread alarm and fear over a variety of threats such as anthrax, smallpox, plague and the ebola virus. Ordinary people, who can do absolutely nothing to defend themselves against these threats, have been terrified.

Why did they do this?

The only sensible conclusion is that all this scaremongering is being done for a reason. Could that reason be that the Government wants to bring in new, even more restrictive laws on the back of all this fear?

80

The Americans have given the words 'prejudice' and 'repression' new meaning. And other countries have blindly followed the American way. The British Government wants to pass a new law giving it the authority to pass into British law any new crime legislation that may be agreed in Brussels – without taking the proposed legislation through the House of Commons.

81

'The vast majority of our imports come from outside the country.'
George W. Bush, president of the USA, proving that he has the sort of grasp of economics, politics and geography that one would expect of a 21st Century American president.

82

The USA, the richest country in the world, is one of the world's worst at treating poverty. It has one of the highest infant mortality rates in the so-called civilised world and one of the lowest life expectancy rates. A quarter of the population has no health care and a higher proportion of its citizens are in prison than just about anywhere else.

83

American citizens use (and waste) more energy than those of any other country – and cause more pollution of the environment and the atmosphere than the rest of the world put together.

84

There are many decent, honest, wise Americans. (I know some and value their friendship). But America has to change. It is, without a doubt, currently (and deservedly) the most unpopular nation in the world. The world hates America, and it does so with good cause.

85

The Americans arrested a German, who happened to be in Denmark at the time, for producing a web site which broke American laws but did not break Danish or German laws. The Americans took the German back to the USA to be tried in an American court.

The Americans have a long history of brutish behaviour under similar circumstances. They will simply take a citizen out of a country, take him back to America, try him and put him into an American prison.

(It is perhaps hardly surprising that American prisons are widely acknowledged to be among the most over-crowded and most barbaric in the world.)

86

More than 1.4 million black Americans (13 per cent of all the black males in America) have permanently lost their right to vote because they have been imprisoned for using drugs. Yet another fine example of American democracy in action.

87

An American poll shows that a large proportion of the American public think that their government is corrupt, secretive and conspiratorial. The poll, conducted by Ohio University and the Scripps Howard News Service found that:

a) 51 per cent of Americans believe it likely that federal officials were directly responsible for president Kennedy's assassination.
b) More than 33 per cent of Americans suspect that the USA Navy shot down TWA flight 800 either on purpose or by accident.
c) Nearly 50 per cent of Americans suspect that FBI agents deliberately started the fires that killed 81 Branch Davidians near Waco, Texas in 1993.
d) 60 per cent of Americans believe that the USA Government is withholding information about military abuses in the Vietnam and Gulf Wars.
e) More than 50 per cent of Americans believe it is possible that the CIA intentionally permitted Central American drug dealers to sell cocaine to inner city black children in the USA.

A leading American politician commented: 'When we believe that our free institutions can commonly be corrupted to dark and evil purposes it is a statement of a feeling of helplessness. We are in for some turbulent years ahead as a nation.'

88

George W. Bush wants a war against Iraq because America wants the oil. But he also wants another war because his campaign in Afghanistan had been a total disaster. After six months of bombing and occupation he still hadn't even found his main target, Osama bin Laden. He killed thousands of innocent citizens, destroyed what there was of the nation's infrastructure, overthrew the government and replaced it with anarchy.

America isn't in the slightest bit interested in whether Saddam Hussein has or has not been a 'bad leader', or how badly he has mistreated some of his citizens.

Bush's alleged reason for invading Iraq is that it is a threat to international security. In practice, Israel would be a more sensible target. Sharon and the aggressive Israelis are a far greater threat to world peace than Saddam Hussein. (The Israelis were, not surprisingly, enthusiastic supporters of Bush's plan for a war against Iraq. When Tony Blair invited 18 religious leaders to Number 10 Downing Street, in order to try to gain their support for a war he claimed was 'moral', the only religious leader to support the Bush 'n' Blair policy on Iraq was Chief Rabbi Jonathan Sacks.)

George W. Bush wants to avenge his Dad's error in pulling out of Iraq last time – despite the risk that this will increase calls for a Muslim holy war.

89

'Three words describe modern America: corrupt, cruel and conceited.'
READER'S LETTER

90

The American bombing of retreating, surrendering Iraqi troops at the end of the Gulf War – despite the fact that the retreating Iraqis were waving white flags – was one of the most cowardly and disgraceful acts of war ever seen.

91

No one really believes that George W. Bush is driving the Americans to war. He is sitting in the front and he's the one giving the orders and the interviews. But the mad, out of control drive to war is being manipulated from the back seat by neo-conservatives who are strongly religious and who believe that Iraq is a genuine threat to Israel. These individuals are committed to removing Saddam Hussein; to interfering in the leadership of a foreign country and obtaining a 'regime change'. They see only the short term picture. They do not see the long term consequences of their actions. I doubt very much if Israel itself is pushing for a war against Iraq. Israeli politicians probably understand Middle East politics rather better than American politicians. They know that the destabilisation of the Middle East would, in the medium to long term, result in the destruction of Israel. As one independent commentator recently put it: 'some of Israel's worst enemies are pro-Israeli Americans'.

92

'Why are Americans so bad at spelling?'
NINE-YEAR-OLD READER'S LETTER

93

George W. Bush invested $606,000 of borrowed money in a baseball team called the Texas Rangers. The investment made him popular locally and helped him become State Governor of Texas. He and his fellow investors were then given a $135 million subsidy by local taxpayers so that they could build a new stadium. Bush then sold out and pocketed $14.9 million. That was George W. Bush's first big money making project.

94

The Americans, though they may be bullies at heart, are not good at wars and they are not good in crises. Who, other than the Americans, could have put the New York City Emergency Command

Bunker on the 23rd floor of the World Trade Centre – a building which had already been bombed once before?

95

The American people are, by and large, an insular and parochial lot. Nine out of ten of them don't even have passports. They won't travel outside America for 'security reasons'. (Ignoring the fact that gun happy America is the most dangerous and violent country in the world.) Most Americans simply don't understand (or accept) that they are disliked (or even hated) by much of the rest of the world.

'How can anyone hate America?' asked an American commentator, apparently quite seriously, not realising that to anyone not an American 'How can anyone not hate America?' would have been a more sensible question.

The truth is that America is disliked for all sorts of reasons.

The Americans themselves suspect that when people hate them it is because of envy.

Wrong.

Relatively few people outside the USA envy the American way of life.

But there is much resentment.

There is resentment about the fact that the Americans are taking seeds which have been grown for centuries and claiming ownership; there is resentment about the fact that the Americans are forcing their genetically engineered food onto the world; there is resentment about the fact that the Americans have ruined the world climate in order to keep their own oil industry happy; there is resentment about the fact that although the USA is the world's biggest polluter it imposes the lowest restrictions and taxes on polluters of any industrial nation.

America always thinks first of itself. It is like an overgrown teenager with over-indulgent parents. Too much money. Too much brute strength. But not enough wisdom and not enough subtlety. And not enough consideration for others.

96

Other leaders around the world (particularly British) are so desperate to suck up to the Americans (the wealthy school bully) that they seem happy to denigrate their own citizens. In the UK it was decided that there should be a three minute silence on Friday 14th September in memory of the dead. Why three minutes? It is usual for British servicemen to get one minute. Are Americans three times as valuable as British servicemen?

If we had three minute silences every time a nation loses several thousand citizens in a disaster of some sort we would be all living like Trappist monks.

97

George W. Bush and his cronies claim to be protecting our freedom. But they are removing our freedom not protecting it. The new laws being introduced on both sides of the Atlantic are being brought in to eradicate our freedom and to stop campaigners.

98

American style politics (all spin and no substance) is spreading around the world. Tony Blair's New Labour government is Britain's first American style government. Blair and his colleagues took advice on how to win an election from cigar smoker and USA president Bill Clinton. Tony Blair probably knew Clinton before Monica Lewinsky did.

99

Bush is the bad guy, the global terrorist; waging war for territorial gain (oil fields).

100

The Americans claim that giving hormones to cattle is perfectly safe. When beef from such cattle was banned in the EU the Americans responded by banning some European imports (more out of governmental spite than through any sense of commercial logic).

American farmers give six sex hormones to their cattle for exactly the same reason that body-builders and weight lifters take hormones: to build more muscle. The benefit to a farmer is financial: there is obviously more saleable beef on a heavily muscled cow.

The row, which has been going on for well over a decade, is about whether or not beef taken from cows which have been given extra hormones is safe to eat. Although there is no evidence to show that hormone soaked beef is safe, American farmers say that it is. And that, of course, is good enough for their government.

However, European farmers are not allowed to give extra hormones to cattle. And so, not surprisingly, they have put pressure on European politicians to ban the American beef (which, because of the help from the hormones, is cheaper to produce).

The American claim that it is safe to give hormones to cattle is based upon the fact that there is, as yet, not very much scientific proof that it is dangerous to do this. This is exactly the same spurious argument that is used to defend genetic engineering, microwave ovens and other possible hazards to human health.

Everyone conveniently ignores the fact that it is extremely difficult to prove that something is dangerous when little or no research has been done to find the truth.

What we do know, however, is that there can be a greater amount of sex hormones in 500 grams of American meat than a pubertal boy produces in a day. And that's a lot. And sex hormones can and do have a dramatic effect on any human body (and mind).

Moreover, research has been done showing that there is a convincing epidemiological link between one of the six hormones used by American farmers, and endometrial and breast cancers. The hormone causes cancer by interfering with a cell's DNA – a process known as genotoxicity. It is generally accepted that there are no safe levels for genotoxic substances.

You might think that would be enough to embarrass the American politicians into telling their farmers to stop using hormones.

After all, the incidence of cancer is rising dramatically in the USA – and has been doing so for some years.

However, the American farmers (and their Government) have taken comfort from the fact that although a joint committee set up by the World Health Organisation and the Food and Agriculture Organisation has agreed that one of the hormones in use (estradiol-17-beta) has what it calls 'genotoxic properties', and does cause cancer, it has argued that it is safe to allow people to consume modest amounts of this cancer inducing hormone. Moreover, much to the delight of the Americans, the committee claims to know what the safe level is. You will not be surprised to hear that the American farmers and their government claim that their beef contains a safe amount of this known cancer inducing substance.

Anyone who eats American beef is playing a modern version of Russian roulette and is exhibiting an extraordinary amount of trust in a group of people (American politicians and American farmers) who have consistently shown that they do not give a fig for human health or human life.

101

What is happening to our freedom? That's the big question.

The subsidiary questions are:

1) Are the events of September 11th being used as an excuse for a dramatic extension of government powers?

2) Were the events of September 11th deliberately organised (or allowed to occur) by Western governments – knowing that they could use them as a cover to introduce restrictive new laws?

The answer to the first question is a definite 'yes'. And the answer to the second question is 'almost certainly'.

102

Americans have yet to learn (and it is clearly going to be a long, painful journey) that you cannot force people to admire and respect you. They have yet to learn that you cannot crush rebels and revolutionaries who are prepared to die to defeat you.

103

Just like the British Government, the American Government is erod-
ing civil liberties rapidly and is using the war on terrorism as the
excuse. In the aftermath of the September 11th attacks the American Pentagon opened its Total Information Awareness project.

New software trawls through commercial and government computer databases in search of suspicious patterns which might suggest that a terrorist is at work.

Of course, in order to identify possibly conspiratorial behaviour involving a few individuals the computers must sift through
the personal information of tens of millions of ordinary, innocent,
law abiding citizens – with neither their knowledge nor their consent. As a result of the new software, the USA Government can
now keep track of every citizen's movements.

The leader of this special project is retired Navy Admiral John
Poindexter, perhaps still best known for the fact that he was convicted of lying to the USA Congress about the Reagan administration's plans to use profits from Iranian arms sales to fund rebels in
Nicaragua. (Poindexter was found guilty of conspiracy, obstruction
of justice and the destruction of evidence and though his convic-
tion was later overturned in the USA he has been banned from
entering Costa Rica.)

The Pentagon's new project (the motto of which is 'Knowledge
is Power') has as its logo a picture of the globe being watched by a
pyramid topped with the eye of God – a symbol guaranteed to
breathe fire into the hearts of all conspiracy theorists.

The plans for the project were not shared with ordinary American politicians since the details were initially buried in a 'technology development' budget.

(In addition to giving Poindexter an important post in his Government, George W. Bush has also employed other men who were
discredited in the Iran-Contra affair. For example, Elliot Abrams
was appointed Director of the National Security Council's Office
for Democracy, Human Rights and International Relations despite
the fact that in 1991 he pleaded guilty to withholding evidence
from Congress about his role in the Iran-Contra affair. It has been
alleged that Abrams was responsible for covering up atrocities committed by USA sponsored Contras. Atrocities committed by the

Contras included the raping, torturing and killing of unarmed civilians, including children and the blinding, dismembering, burning and beheading of groups of civilians, including women and children. Abrams was pardoned by George W. Bush's father, former USA president George Bush.)

104

'The American people, taking one with another, constitute the most timorous, snivelling, poltroonish, ignominious mob of serfs and goosesteppers ever gathered under one flag in Christendom since the end of the Middle Ages.'
H. L. MENCKEN

105

America finds it impossible to accept criticism – even from within. Gore Vidal, one of America's most eminent and successful authors, wrote an essay after 11/9 explaining why America got to be so hated. 'I thought it useful,' he wrote, 'to describe the various provocations on our side that drove them (Osama bin Laden and others) to such terrible acts.' American publishers refused to publish the essay, which subsequently appeared in a book entitled *Perpetual War for Perpetual Peace*. (Vidal's book, subtitled *How We Got To Be So Hated – Causes Of Conflict In The Last Empire*, was eventually published in the United Kingdom. When made available to Americans, it sold 100,000 copies in the USA)

106

American arms companies design and manufacture cluster bombs to be dropped on undefended villages. They also manufacture landmines which are specifically intended to maim small children.

107

George W. Bush and his family and advisors, will, of course, be safe and well protected from the activities of terrorists inspired by America's war on terrorism.

108

Within days of September 11th, the British Home Office had announced that it was re-evaluating concessions made to business and civil liberties lobbyists and was planning to give security agencies authority to intercept all private e-mails – including encrypted and internet files, and forcing all companies to give decryption keys to a central government run repository.

Store your files on the internet, or have a computer connected to the internet, and the chances that wherever you live one or more governments can and will now read whatever you write and check up on your contacts, your investments, your bank deposits and your hobbies without you being any the wiser.

109

Bank secrecy and privacy are being made illegal in the name of hunting down terrorists. The truth is that laws opposing bank secrecy make no difference whatsoever to terrorists. But they make it easier for governments to control and tax their citizens.

The world has changed. But who changed it? And why?

110

Once upon a time, George W. Bush had shares in an oil company called Harken Energy. He was also made chairman of the company. George's daddy was president of the USA at the time. Harken got an offshore drilling deal in Bahrain. In the summer of 1990,

George W. Bush sold most of his shares in Harken and more than doubled his investment. Iraq invaded Kuwait just six weeks later. And then a short while after that George's daddy invaded Iraq. (There have been suggestions that the CIA was involved and may have encouraged Iraq to invade Kuwait in the first place.)

When Iraq invaded Kuwait the value of the Harken shares fell sharply. Harken then announced unprecedented losses. The shares fell still further.

George W. Bush waited eight months before telling America's Securities and Exchange Commission that he had sold his stock.

After an investigation which lasted for years the SEC eventually told George's lawyer that no further action was planned 'at the present time'.

There was a lack of evidence of any wrong doing.

111

The State of Mississippi is reported to be in default on $7 million worth of bonds. The state borrowed the money in the 1830s to provide capital for two banks but in 1841 the governor of the state repudiated the bonds claiming that: 'the toiling millions never should be burdened with taxes to support the idle few'. Mississippi eventually amended its own constitution (contrary to the section in the USA constitution which forbids states from passing laws impairing contractual obligations) to protect itself from ever having to fulfil its contractual obligations.

In 1934 bondholders gave some bonds to the principality of Monaco so that Monaco could sue the state (the USA constitution forbids citizens of other countries from suing the states). But the Supreme Court refused to hear the case on the grounds that a state could not be sued without its consent. Not surprisingly, Mississippi did not consent to being sued.

Some American citizens then tried to sue Mississippi but in 1996 a court ruled that the bondholders' right to sue expired in 1880. Mississippi has never paid what it owes to the bondholders.

112

'Inappropriate comments are illegal.'
SIGN SEEN IN AMERICAN AIRPORTS.

113

Were American agents in any way involved with the plane crash at Lockerbie?

114

George W. Bush claims that he is fighting a war for freedom. He's not. He's waging a war to prevent us noticing that we don't have any freedom, and that our rights are disappearing faster than snow in sunshine.

The American Government doesn't give a fig for you or your family, for your safety or for your freedom. The American Government is packed with world class hypocrites, liars and cheats.

Bush has decided that we will all be at war until terrorism and evil have been eradicated.

Do these unreal and impractical aims remind you of anything? They should. The discredited, pointless and unsuccessful Drugs War.

Bush tells us that this war is all about freedom.

But how can we be fighting for freedom if they've already taken our freedom away from us?

115

Despite being financially and politically committed to the EU, Britain has been turning its back on its European allies for some time now.

After the war in Yugoslavia Britain severed many of its ties with France, Germany and Italy and allied itself with the USA. The USA and the UK want to ensure the dominance of their defence contractors and oil companies and to establish control over strategic pipelines through and from the Balkans, Eastern Europe and the former USSR.

At one point the American Government is claimed to have deliberately destabilised Macedonia in order to allow easier access for an oil pipeline jointly owned by the USA and the UK.

In Yugoslavia the Americans (with New Labour support from the UK) managed to renew violence between ethnic groups, to provoke a humanitarian catastrophe and to destabilise the Balkans.

116

Bush's new permanent war is being fought to distract us from the real issues. Every day of every week of every month of every year more than 21,000 people die unnecessarily. They die in terror and in pain. Every day – every single day – six times as many people are callously killed by the world's large corporations as were killed by whichever band of terrorists attacked America on September 11th. Today, tomorrow and every day.

The truth is that Bush, and his faithful puppy Blair, are fighting the wrong war. There is a bigger war they should be fighting. And that's a war against the greed of global capitalism (led by corporate America). That's the war which would truly save millions of lives, make the world a better place and enable more people to enjoy physical, mental and spiritual good health.

But that's a war Bush will never fight. Because he's part of the problem.

Look at the big issues – and what our so-called leaders are doing to deal with them.

1. Every year several million people in America and Europe die from cancer. Unless they are hideously ignorant Bush and Blair both know what causes eight out of ten cancers; they therefore know that the vast majority of cancers are preventable. Simply persuading people to stop eating meat would save millions of lives. There is no little irony in the fact that if anti-American feeling results in the closure of fast food outlets worldwide (the word 'restaurants' seems inappropriate) tens of thousands of lives will be saved. If Bush 'n' Blair are properly briefed they also know that

current methods of cancer treatment are destructive and ineffective – and that the cancer industry has consistently suppressed new therapies which might (and possibly do) work.

What is Bush doing about this? Nothing. Actually, less than nothing. The American Government (like the EU) still subsidises the growing of tobacco. There seems little point in spending small amounts trying to stop people smoking if you are spending large amounts encouraging them to do so by making it cheaper than it would otherwise be. Only 5 per cent of the $246 billion tobacco settlement handed over by tobacco companies in the USA has been used on campaigns to stop people smoking. American states are just as hooked on tobacco as are their citizens (and as politicians in Europe). If people smoke less, taxes will fall and there will be more people living long enough to claim their pensions. It's easy to understand why politicians don't want tobacco smoking stopped. It's difficult to understand how or why they get away with it.

Who benefits? Tobacco and chemical companies whose products cause those cancers and drug companies (often subsidiaries of the chemical companies) who make the drugs which are sold to treat the cancers (but which do not work).

Who loses? You, your family and your friends.

2. Heart disease is a major killer. Every day far more people die from heart disease than died as a result of the terrorist attack on September 11th. Most cases of heart disease could be prevented. Most people with heart disease can be cured with a simple regime which costs almost nothing to follow and which is more effective than drugs and surgery.

Bush and Blair should know this but what are they doing about it? Nothing.

Who benefits? Food and tobacco companies. And drug companies.

Who loses? You, your family and your friends.

3. Bush (and Blair) should know that the so-called drinking water you get out of your tap is full of chemicals. What do these chemicals do to your body? Who knows?

What are our leaders doing about this? Nothing.

Who benefits? Big water companies.

Who loses? You, your family and your friends.

4. Infectious diseases are coming back in a big way. Antibiotics

are no longer effective. One reason is that farmers are allowed to put antibiotics into animal feed to boost farm profits.

What are Bush and Blair doing about this? Nothing.

Who benefits? Drug companies and farmers.

Who loses? You, your family and your friends.

5. The food available in our shops is so bereft of essential ingredients that in order to stay healthy we all need to swallow vitamin and mineral supplements.

What are Bush and Blair doing about this? Nothing.

Who benefits? Farmers and food companies.

Who loses? You, your family and your friends.

Of course terrorism is bad. But allowing people to die unnecessarily of cancer, heart disease and infectious diseases is also wrong. It is just as wrong. The people who die of cancer and heart disease will suffer more than the people who die suddenly in a terrorist explosion. The mourning of relatives and friends will be just as real.

All unnecessary deaths are awful – both for those who die and for those who are left behind. We should be doing everything we can to prevent them.

Our governments have chosen to put all their current (and, probably, future) effort into one target – terrorism – which suits them and which will not cost them corporate friends.

Bush isn't fighting this unending war to preserve our freedom. He is fighting this unending war for money and for oil. And he is fighting this war to distract us from the real wars we should be fighting.

Deaths from cancer and heart disease are not usually dramatic. People who die from these diseases don't die on television. They don't become heroes.

But cancer and heart disease are a much bigger threat to most families than terrorism will ever be.

Bush and Blair are fighting the wrong war. If they cared about people – you and I – they would be fighting the global corporations which are destroying the world – and creating injustice, frustration, poverty, pain and illness on a massive scale – both among Christians and Muslims. They should be fighting the global corporations which are knowingly killing millions through their ruthlessly wicked profit making policies. But Bush 'n' Blair won't fight that war. For them the price (in lost perks and campaign contributions) would be far too high.

The ultimate irony is surely the fact that if this world really needs a war then multi-national corporations should be on one side – led by Bush 'n' Blair.

And the rest of us – Muslims and Christians – should be fighting shoulder to shoulder against them.

Bush, Blair and other leaders have for years turned a blind eye to the world's real problems. They have forsaken the sick, the dying, the hungry and the bereaved so as not to distress their corporate masters.

Now they want to us to cheer them on in a war very few people understand, that will probably never end and that isn't even just. They want us to cheer when our armies drop bombs on innocent citizens in revenge for one day of terrorism in the USA. But they will do nothing to protect us from the very real threats which hang over our lives.

117

'It's amazing I won. I was running against peace, prosperity and incumbency.'
USA PRESIDENT GEORGE W. BUSH, IN AN HONEST MOMENT. BUSH WAS SPEAKING TO SWEDISH PRIME MINISTER GORAN PERRSON, UNAWARE THAT A LIVE TELEVISION CAMERA WAS STILL ROLLING.

118

Mark Twain's masterpiece *Huckleberry Finn*, acknowledged to be one of the greatest anti-racist books ever written, is now banned in the USA because it contains a word which is considered unacceptable by the politically correct. Since most dictionaries contain the word one wonders when Americans will ban dictionaries.

119

During the 2000 presidential campaign, vice president-to-be Dick Cheney, denied that Halliburton Industries, the oil services company that he was C.E.O. of between Bush regimes, had a 'relationship' with Saddam. But in June 2001 it was revealed in that two Halliburton subsidiaries were doing business with Saddam. Sanctions which prevented Iraq from purchasing water purification equipment clearly did not apply to Halliburton. Under George Bush senior Dick Cheney was defence secretary, in charge of the military campaign during the Gulf War. As America prepared to destroy Iraq in 2003, the USA Defence Department said Halliburton was included in its plans.

120

USA president George W. Bush's predecessor was just as committed to intervention as George himself clearly is. President Bill Clinton was an enthusiastic supporter of the Northern Ireland peace process. It is difficult to see exactly what 'peace' has come out of this but the process has resulted in the release of many of those who were arrested for threatening the 'peace' in the first place. Paramilitary commanders have been rewarded with executive positions in the local Government. Very few, if any, weapons were surrendered during the Clinton and Blair peace process.

121

'In addition to wanting to get their hands on the oil the Americans want to attack Iraq in order to protect Israel. Iraq probably does want to destroy Israel, largely because of its aggression towards the Palestinians. It would, of course, have made more sense to persuade the Israelis to behave more reasonably towards the Palestinians. But that wouldn't win any American votes or please rich Jewish presidential backers in the USA. Attacking Iraq will unite Muslims against Christians. Dealing with Israel would have solved one of the world's primary threats to peace.'
READER'S LETTER

122

'...the nightmare of American hysteria, ignorance, arrogance, stupidity and belligerence: the most powerful nation the world has ever known effectively waging war against the rest of the world.'
HAROLD PINTER

123

It was always obvious that other governments would use America's war of revenge as an excuse to introduce new constraints on our rapidly diminishing freedom. The American and British Governments have made fascism, racism and warmongering fashionable.

Britain's Prime Minister Blair has told the world that he is going to eradicate terrorism completely. An equally improbable Bush has promised to 'rid the world of evil'. Newspapers and TV have been crammed with jingoistic echoes.

The truth is that for years we have been losing more and more of our freedom and our privacy.

For example, Britain already has more CCTV cameras than any other nation on earth. Nothing is confidential. The Government and local authorities in the UK have spent £1 billion of taxpayers' money on CCTV cameras over the last decade. There are now far more CCTV cameras in the UK than in any other country on the planet. Lots more are planned. A whole industry has developed around these cameras and countless thousands of people are employed to watch the 24 hour coverage they provide. Most Britons seem unconcerned about this gross invasion of their privacy even though there is absolutely no evidence that these cameras reduce crime, reduce anxiety about crime or help solve crimes. Despite having more CCTV cameras than any other country in the world Britain now has the worst crime rate in the world.

What next? Street microphones? Don't laugh. They've already got microphones on the streets in Redwood City, California USA and in Los Angeles USA. Other American cities are planning to follow suit. The courts now accept that when in public places individuals have no reasonable expectation of privacy. The authorities can, and will, peep inside your bag and your pockets without you being aware of it. Actually you don't have much privacy in your home either. In parts of the USA they are now using thermal imaging to see into people's homes. 'They' can see exactly what you're doing.

Our loss of privacy has intensified in recent years. And, with the war on terrorism as an excuse, things are about to get much, much worse. Governments everywhere will be monitoring the movements of terrorists, eavesdropping on their telephone calls and opening their e-mails. To do this they will, of course, have to invade our privacy too. Actually they're already doing it. It's just that now that they have a good excuse any remaining worries about civil liberty are being ignored.

The Echelon system, governed by five English speaking nations (the UK, USA, Australia, Canada and New Zealand) and run by America's National Security Agency uses satellites to eavesdrop on any electronic communication.

Echelon works by recognising key words from its dictionary of trigger words and phrases. Use the wrong word – and it's very easy to do so in an entirely innocent conversation – and you're likely to have armed policemen banging on your door at 4.00 am. Of course, none of this is really much good in the war against terrorists since terrorists are pretty careful about how they communicate with one another. Is there any evidence that this enormously intrusive and expensive system has ever been of practical use in stopping terrorists? No. But never mind. The system is good for keeping an eye on law-abiding citizens. And on companies too. In 1997 the European Parliament ordered an investigation into Echelon after the USA was accused of using its intelligence capabilities to steal international trade secrets. From its European allies, naturally.

It is, of course, possible to encrypt your e-mails. It is possible to purchase programmes so good that it would take 4,000 years for every computer in the USA, working together, to crack the codes they create. But there's a snag. Encrypt your e-mails and the authorities will assume you've got something to hide. They might not be able to read your e-mail messages but you will have attracted their attention; they will watch you closely and, if they decide that they want to read your e-mails they'll force you to hand over the key. To teach you a lesson, and use you as a warning to others who might be tempted to try encryption, you could well find yourself getting one of those 4 .00 am visits from armed policemen. Use e-mail and they'll find you – just as surely and as quickly as if you use a mobile phone. The bottom line: e-mail encryption is pretty much a waste of time. Don't bother.

(The irony here is that British prime minister Tony Blair spends a good deal of time complaining about the press intruding upon his, and his family's, privacy.)

124

In 1998 USA president Bill Clinton unilaterally withdrew weapons inspectors from Iraq in order to prepare the way for a bombing campaign. This was done without getting permission from the United Nations Security Council. By an amazing coincidence, this bombing campaign took place at the same time as (and therefore, sadly, distracted from) president Clinton's impeachment hearings. It is not known how many thousand innocent Iraqis died during this campaign.

125

'War in Iraq: Bush, Rumsfield, Cheney, CIA. Who is manipulating who?'
Placard in Paris 2003

126

Americans should remember that Britain once had far more world power than the USA has now. Hubris comes before a fall. Britain (like France and Spain) had great empires, but declined, slowly, over many decades, because of what it called 'imperial overstretch'. These great powers were eventually unable to finance their extensive military operations. America's economic problems at home suggest that the USA is making exactly the same mistake.

127

Americans think that their relationship with the UK is strong. It isn't. Most Britons loathe the Americans just as much as the French do. The Americans don't see this because they hear and see only what they want to hear and see. The thing the British hate most about America is the way Americans go on and on about 'having saved our asses twice'. America joined both world wars because it had no choice, but it made sure that it benefited enormously as a result. In the Second World War Stalin's USSR did far more than America to help the allied cause.

128

Within the next half century, America will be toppled from its position as world superpower. It will be replaced by China. The Chinese are not awed by the Americans. China has more people and more long-term economic muscle. The Chinese are patient and clever and will wait for the right moment. The Americans probably won't even realise what has happened until it is too late.

129

'We can say unequivocally that the industrial infrastructure needed by Iraq to produce nuclear weapons had been eliminated.'
SCOTT RITTER, FORMER UN WEAPONS INSPECTOR

130

The Americans never supported the British against the IRA. (Indeed, it was they not Gaddafi who were the major source of funding to the terrorists who killed so many Britons.) America did nothing to help the UK after IRA terrorists tried to murder the British Cabinet in 1984 and the Prime Minister in 1991. Indeed the Americans continued to support the IRA. Some 'special relationship'.

131

A new global trade agreement organised by America will privatise most government provided public services and will allow international corporations to run those services for profit. The General Agreement on Trade in Services (GATS) was established in 1994 and was adopted by the World Trade Organisation in 1995.

GATS is a free trade agreement which will 'liberalise' social services and public welfare provided by governments. When GATS is fully implemented it will entitle international corporations to profit from the privatisation of schools, child care, health care, postal services, air and water supplies, public transport, museums and libraries.

GATS will make it illegal for any government to go back to providing publicly owned, non profit making services.

In America, Health Management Organisations are now widespread and Educational Management Organisations (EMOs) are springing up rapidly. The aim of these organisations is, of course, profitability rather than providing a public service. GATS officials want restrictions which will limit any government's ability to bring in environmental and health laws which might hinder 'free trade'.

The World Trade Organisation is, of course, widely acknowledged to be controlled by the USA.

132

'Outside of the killings, Washington DC has one of the lowest crime rates in the USA'
MAYOR MARION BERRY

133

The North American Free Trade Agreement gives international corporations the right to sue governments for lost profits. Potential future profits can also be claimed and, astonishingly, new laws or regulations which are imposed to protect the public interest can lead to compensation. For example, in Mexico a company won a lawsuit against the Mexican government and will receive $16.7 million of Mexican taxpayers' money in compensation for 'profits lost because the (Mexican) Government stopped it building a toxic waste dump.'.

134

A friend with an office in Costa Rica reports that many Americans who contact him try to dial using the Costa Rica international dialling code as an internal state code. He discovered that the Americans did not realise that Costa Rica was a country.

135

Cherie Blair and Laura Bush (wives of UK and USA presidents Blair and Bush) spoke out about the way women in Afghanistan were mistreated by the Taliban. While acknowledging that women were treated unjustly by the Taliban the relevance of this escapes me. Is it now American (and British) policy to carpet-bomb countries which don't let women wear bikinis and listen to rock music? Is it now USA policy to exterminate citizens in countries selected by the President's wife? If human rights violations are a justification for war where will it all end?

Unless the plan is simply to humiliate and provoke Muslims, Cherie and Laura should not stick their undoubtedly perfectly powdered little noses into issues that do not concern them. (Incidentally, shortly after this joint announcement the two husbands welcomed China into the WTO.)

136

In 2003 more than half the British population said they thought that America was an imperialist, bullying nation. The majority of electors said they thought that America was intent on invading Iraq for its own purposes and George Bush was deemed to be just as much of a threat to world peace as Saddam Hussein.

137

Americans leads the world in one area: a breakdown in moral values.

These days American politicians, businessmen and sportsmen all regard 'cheating' as an essential and inevitable part of the recipe for success.

American immorality is now spreading around the world.

138

Politicians in the Soviet Union, the United States of America, Europe and just about everywhere else have for many years dealt with their opponents by 'marginalising' them – or pushing them outside the rest of society by simplifying and falsifying the issues and the facts. Politicians use this technique regularly to control and minimise the effect of those who oppose them, and who might be considered a threat.

Marginalisation is not a new technique. It was used with great effect in the 1930s in the USA where steel firm bosses were having a great deal of difficulty with striking steelworkers. Having found that breaking heads and bones tended to antagonise the public, the steel bosses decided to use the media as a subtle alternative. The argument they used was that strikes (and strikers) were hurting everyone. Union activity was equated with communism. Newspapers were used to tell ordinary citizens that the strikers were damaging their future, their children and their country. 'Striking is un-American', said the bosses.

The simple but extremely effective technique of marginalisation – which usually relies on triggering an instinctive or emotional response – is used by governments whenever they are at war. Anyone who speaks out against any sort of military conflict will quickly be attacked as being 'against our troops' and 'putting our boys lives in danger'.

During the Gulf War anyone who spoke up and complained that the war was only being fought to help keep down the price of oil was accused of 'endangering our troops' and of being 'unpatriotic'. Instead of attempting to explain or justify the war the politicians produced simple slogans such as 'support our troops'. The electors were not given a chance to discuss the war and anyone who dared to point out that modern wars do seem to break out at convenient times for politicians (when an election is due, when there has been a dip in the polls or when a scandal is breaking) was quickly marginalised as 'unpatriotic'.

Much the same thing happened in 2003. Anyone who dared to question the need for war was accused of being unpatriotic and reminded of 'our boys in the desert'. One newspaper editor told me none if his contributors would be allowed to question the need for war once fighting had started. Hypocrisy is encouraged and all moral and legal objections have to be shelved.

Marginalisation claims and accusations work by turning the rest of the community against the targeted individuals or groups. Protesters and dissidents are made to feel alone; members of a tiny, out of step and insignificant minority.

139

An Egyptian newspaper has claimed that during the war in Afghanistan the Americans dropped humanitarian food aid in areas which had been heavily landmined.

140

The Americans can't spell 'defence'. Even apparently educated Americans get it wrong and spell it 'defense'. But they define 'defence' differently too. They seem to get it confused with aggression.

141

America's insistence that the war against Iraq is not about oil has become something of a 'black pantomime'. Every time the Americans say that the war isn't about oil, their voices are drowned by a loud, international chorus of: 'Oh yes it is!'

142

'In war...let your great object be victory, not lengthy campaigns.'
SUN TZU, *THE ART OF WAR*

143

When the Americans attacked Iraq in the Gulf War they deliberately bombed the country's water supplies. Then, after the 'end' of the war the USA helped ensure that new water purification systems could not be imported into Iraq.

The result is that thousands of innocent Iraqis (including young children) have died. The United Nations estimates that more than over a million citizens (including 500,000 Iraqi children) have died as a direct result of the sanctions against Iraq and that unclean water is a major contributor to these deaths.

The American Pentagon knew of, and monitored, the destruction of Iraq's water supplies, despite the fact that the destruction of civilian infrastructures which are essential for health and welfare is in direct violation of the Geneva Convention.

The American Government knew that bacteria develop in unpurified water, that epidemics would occur, that the manufacture of safe medicine would be compromised, that food supplies would be affected and that, as a result, there would be thousands of civilian deaths.

The United States of America has deliberately violated the Geneva Convention.

(It is reasonable to say that none of this has helped improve the image of America in the Arab world.)

144

The Americans are the most parochial people in the world. Surveys repeatedly show that most Americans have no idea where other countries are or who leads them.

145

'Today America's allies worry about a new threat – America...they worry about living in an American-dominated world in which their national destinies are shaped by Washington.'
NEWSWEEK MAGAZINE

146

'American parochialism makes it impossible for Americans to understand other nations. It is their parochialism which explains why their military adventures abroad (think of Korea and Vietnam, for example) have been so spectacularly unsuccessful. The Americans like to think of themselves as warriors but when it comes to war they are definitely stuck in the lower reaches of the third division.'
READER'S LETTER

147

Democratic citizenship is being undermined by America. Workers in Malaysia, employed by American companies, were forbidden to organise labour unions. When the Malaysian government suggested lifting this ban the American companies simply threatened to leave. The local government gave in. The multinationals constantly get labour concessions and government hand-outs by threatening to move their factories to other parts of the world.

148

'Our country is wherever we are well off.'
JOHN MILTON WRITING IN 1666 (AND REFERRING TO SPIRITUAL, MORAL AND PHYSICAL WEALTH, RATHER THAN STOCK OPTIONS IN ENRON).

149

War is God's way of teaching Americans geography.

150

The Americans love to claim responsibility for all sorts of things that aren't theirs. For example, *Business Week* magazine recently described steel tycoon and philanthropist Andrew Carnegie as an American industrialist. But Carnegie was born in Scotland not America.

151

'If we don't succeed, we run the risk of failure.'
GEORGE W. BUSH, PRESIDENT OF THE USA, AS INCISIVE AS EVER.

152

The country which gave us burgers and cola drinks has condemned us all to a more polluted, more dangerous future and Bush has ensured that he will be remembered as one of the world's worst leaders.

America is already responsible for one quarter of all the pollution on the planet (and the percentage for which America is responsible is getting higher all the time).

Americans don't care about the Kyoto agreement because quirks of fate mean that global warming will affect America less than other parts of the world.

Other world leaders should respond by introducing a total ban on Americans. Boycotting American goods, refusing to give Americans permission to take part in sporting events and refusing Americans visas to travel would be a good starting point.

153

'He will win who knows when to fight and when not to fight.'
SUN TZU, *THE ART OF WAR*

154

In the name of 'humanitarian intervention' USA president Bill Clinton sent American troops to Bosnia to work with hard-line Islamic fighters who were on record as opposing the idea of peace between Islamic and non-Islamic institutions. When the Americans supported the Kosovan Libertarian Army they may, or may not, have been aware that some of those fighting for Kosovo had links with Al Qaeda, received much of their funding from the marketing of illegal narcotics and were said within the EU to be connected to Albanian drug gangs supplying Western Europe with over three quarters of its heroin. (In addition, Albanian gangs now control over two thirds of the vice trade in Soho.)

155

The UK has now adopted the American habit of everyone suing everyone for just about everything imaginable. An American parent was sued for £175,000 for shaking a teacher's hand too hard. A shoplifter was awarded over £2,000,000 for the 'trauma' of being handcuffed in front on her children. An 81-year-old woman was given £2,000,000 after she spilt hot coffee in her own lap. A burglar who fell through a skylight successfully sued the houseowner.

The American inspired compensation-culture creates an endless stream of victims who do not want to take responsibility for their own lives but expect others to pay for everything bad that happens to them. Every mild moment of misfortune, every cruel twist of fate has to be someone else's fault and there is always a lawyer around to prove that it is.

Most of those who sue for compensation because they have been encouraged to think of themselves as victims are belittling themselves and leading to a steady decline in the strength of our society.

In many cases victories are won because defendants decide that it is cheaper to pay out a small sum than it is to hire lawyers and fight a case. Most of these claims are run through the USA inspired 'no win no fee' system and the majority seem to involve falls on pavements, in supermarkets and at work.

The end result will, of course, be that big businesses will put up prices and a lot of small businesses will go bankrupt. Rapidly and dramatically rising insurance premiums have already led to the demise of many British firms.

Thanks to America almost 5 per cent of Britain's expenditure on health care now goes on lawyers, litigation and legal proceedings.

156

In the Spring of 2003 the Americans announced that they were developing new nuclear weapons in violation of treaties which they had signed. 'This is,' said one eminent commentator, 'clearly a case of 'do as we say not as we do'.'

These plans had originally been revealed in July 2001 when a weapons advocacy group consisting of nuclear scientists, government officials and right wing analysts proposed developing a 'mini-nuke' capable of burrowing into underground weapon supplies and producing a 'contained' nuclear explosion.

The USA Government wants to revive its nuclear weapons programme in order to ensure that it maintains global nuclear domination.

157

There are 110 million landmines buried in the world today. Most of the people at risk are civilians. Many of the landmines are specifically designed to maim children – on the downright barbaric grounds that when children lose limbs the cost to the local community is huge, both in emotional and economic terms. A large proportion of the buried landmines were manufactured and sold by established, government-backed American companies and arms dealers. The American government refuses to outlaw landmines.

158

Those who claim that a war against Iraq is not an attempt by the USA to grab Iraq's oil are surely either blatantly dishonest (and probably bought and paid for by the oil industry), or rather sadly naive.

159

The word 'kakistocracy' means the 'government of the state by the worst citizens'.

160

'We make the finest packaging in the world but the stuff inside is mostly junk.'
RAYMOND CHANDLER

161

The Americans are keen to unite Ireland (and happy to support terrorists there) but their enthusiasm for uniting countries isn't always consistent. Just think of Vietnam and Korea.

162

There are three million Arab-Americans living in the USA and since September 11th they have been subjected to a pretty vile barrage of bigotry and suspicion. Passengers have repeatedly refused to board aeroplanes containing Arab – or Arab looking – passengers. Arabic men, women and children have been attacked in the streets. A Jordanian who was rushed to a hospital in America was taunted by guards in the waiting room. When he responded and a shouting match started the guards handcuffed him, took him to a back room, beat him and stole $450 and his green card from his wallet. They then told him: 'You're not a human. You're an animal. We're going to ship you back where you came from and put you in a cave where you belong.' Would Americans tolerate such treatment of Jews?

163

Eight out of ten Americans can't find Japan on a map. And one in five Americans have no idea where their nation is in relation to other countries.

164

Throughout the racially tense months when America was intent on starting another war against Muslims in general and Iraq in particular (and was being widely criticised for its pro-Israeli policies) the official White House spokesman was an employee called Mr Ari Fleischer. This was a good example of American diplomacy.

165

Of all the commercially viable concepts created since World War II, 5 per cent came from Japan, 25 per cent came from the USA and 56 per cent came from Britain.

166

'The annual American budget for intelligence services is $30 billion. If I was an American taxpayer I would be wondering if I was getting value for money.'
READER'S LETTER

167

In 2003 the United Nations didn't need to send weapons inspectors into Iraq to find out what weapons Saddam Hussein has. All the UN needed to do was to ask the British and American Governments for an inventory. It was the American and British Governments which had provided Iraq with its weapons. (Some of the weapons had been gifts. Some had been sold.)

168

Sixty per cent of Americans aged between 16 and 25 are officially classed as 'functionally illiterate'.

169

The study of fingerprints isn't so much a science as a sort of guessing game. No one really knows whether or not two people might have the same fingerprints. And no one really knows how to identify fingerprints with certainty. As a result the way in which fingerprints are used as evidence varies from country to country. In Italy, for example, the courts require experts to find at least 16 identical features between the fingerprint of an accused and a fingerprint found at a crime scene. In America they aren't so fussy; courts there simply require two fingerprint examiners to 'agree' that there is a match.

170

As America's $37.7 billion Homeland Security Department settles in, so freedom and privacy are disappearing fast, both from within the USA and elsewhere in the world. After one protest demonstration in the USA a Yale professor was detained for 14 hours for talking to reporters and fined $100 for 'failure to obey'.

The Homeland Security Department was, inevitably, set up after the attack of 11/9 (a date which the Americans, for reasons best known to themselves, insist on wrongly referring to as 9/11 which is the 9th of November) and as a result banks in 30 states now require a thumbprint signature from people wanting to do something as provocative as cash a cheque.

Biometric scanning for identification is also becoming popular and hundreds of thousands of Americans have already had their faces, fingers or thumbs scanned. Banks and other businesses are now reported to spy on their customers and to report any suspicious behaviour to their government.

Several American states have enacted the Medical Emergency Health Powers Act and criminalised the refusal to take a state ordered vaccination; though just what this has to do with terrorism or emergencies I am somewhat at a loss to understand. The end result of this is that if a child doesn't have a vaccination that has been deemed necessary by the state then the child and the parent can be fined and sent to prison. Oh, and their property can be confiscated too. And the child can be forcibly vaccinated.

This is the 'land of the free' that Americans are fighting to preserve.

171

If there was a Nobel Prize for War, American president George W. Bush and Tony Blair would be clear, joint winners.

172

Fish farms supply almost all of the trout and catfish, and half of the salmon and shrimp consumed in the USA. Worldwide one third of the seafood consumed is farmed fish.

However, a recent study showed that a single serving of farmed salmon contains three to six times the World Health Organisation's recommended daily intake limit for dioxins.

Farmed salmon (usually known as 'Atlantic salmon') are genetically modified to be larger (and therefore more profitable) than wild salmon. As a result a salmon farm which contains 200,000 fish releases nitrogen, phosphorus and faecal matter roughly equivalent to the untreated sewage from between 20,000 and 25,000 human beings.

One huge problem is that American fish farmers use a wide range of chemicals (including hormones, antibiotics, anaesthetics, pesticides etc.) in order to help increase their profits. The use of antibiotics by fish farmers is a particular hazard since it leads to antibiotic resistance.

173

George W. Bush's Government (allegedly supporters of the free market) has increased farming subsidies to $19 billion a year for the next decade. Cotton subsidies to giant, industrialised farms have risen to $4 billion (slightly excessive perhaps when you realise that the total world market for cotton is worth $3 billion). The American subsidies have killed all export opportunities for 11 million households in West Africa who are reliant on cotton farming.

174

Americans have put 'September 11th 2001' onto their list of the ten most important days in man's history. That is truly absurd and is akin to describing a teen recording artist as 'the greatest singer ever' on the basis of one three minute recording. What happened in America was sad but hardly compares to numerous other events in history. The September 11th incidents were dramatic and memorable (and well documented) but by international standards of disaster they were relatively small incidents. Haven't Americans heard of the Black Death – which killed 25 million people (admittedly all Europeans)? Then there were the two World Wars of the 20th century which killed quite a few. Of course, not having taken much part in the two World Wars, America may feel a little embarrassed about those events, and prefer to ignore them.

175

In March 2003 in Europe, America's war on Iraq was described as 'Bush's Holy War'. There was much agreement that the inarticulate Bush (widely perceived as arrogant and vain) characterised much that millions dislike most about America. It was reported, to no one's surprise, that Bush had agreed to address the European Union on condition that they agreed to give him a standing ovation.

176

Other countries are quickly following America's example in exchanging freedom for 'security'. The European Union is considering fingerprinting or eye scanning every citizen in the E.U. The excuse is that this will help combat terrorism, though no one has yet explained precisely how this will work.

177

Not even British holidaymakers are safe from the Americans these days. As America and Britain prepared to start a war against Iraq the American FBI requested the arrest of a 72-year-old British pensioner on a wine tasting holiday in South Africa, wrongly alleging that he was wanted for fraud in the USA. At the Americans' command the South African police obediently kept the man in prison for three weeks (sleeping on a thin mat on a concrete floor) though it was ten days before anyone bothered to turn up to question him; ten days before anyone bothered to take a statement from him or even ask him who he was. When, eventually, the unfortunate pensioner was released the Americans explained that they had mistaken him for a fraudster they'd just arrested in Las Vegas. The fraudster and the pensioner had different names and according to the *Financial Times* in London a photograph of the suspect posted on an Interpol web site did not closely resemble the British pensioner.

The American authorities collect fingerprints, eye scans, photographs and private information like small boys collect stamps and yet it still took them three weeks to differentiate between an American conman and a British pensioner.

Can you imagine the outcry in the USA if British policemen had told the Mexican police to arrest an American and had then kept him incarcerated needlessly for three weeks?

Is it any wonder that the Americans can't find Osama bin Laden?

(The British Foreign Office, apparently terrified of embarrassing the Americans, apparently spent much of the three weeks trying to persuade the relatives of the arrested pensioner not to go to the press. However, when the relatives eventually did ring the British newspapers, the wrongly arrested man was freed within 48 hours. The lesson here is clear: if you are in trouble abroad ring the media not your local embassy or consulate.)

178

'This coming battle, if it materialises, represents a turning point in USA foreign policy and possibly a turning point in the recent history of the world. This nation is about to embark upon the first test of a revolutionary doctrine applied in an extraordinary way at an unfortunate time. The doctrine of preemption — the idea that the United States or any other nation can legitimately attack a nation that is not imminently threatening but may be threatening in the future — is a radical new twist on the traditional idea of self defence. It appears to be in contravention of international law and the U.N. Charter. And it is being tested at a time of world-wide terrorism, making many countries around the globe wonder if they will soon be on our — or some other nation's — hit list.'

USA SENATOR ROBERT BYRD, SPEAKING IN THE USA
SENATE 12.2.2003

179

'In their treatment of prisoners of war brought back from Afghanistan the Americans have proved themselves to be brutal, cruel and in humane. Forcibly shaving off the beards and hair of their prisoners, shackling them and throwing them into metal cages was something

Hitler's concentration camp guards would surely have been proud of.
It will be no good Americans whingeing (as they will) when
American servicemen are captured and treated cruelly and brutally.
The Americans, incidentally, didn't even have the bottle to keep
their prisoners on USA soil.'

180

'Trick or treat' originated in Ireland as a pleasant enough Halloween tradition. Just a bit of fun. The Americans, as is their way, added greed and the threat of violence and turned an innocent (if pagan) festival into something scary and unwholesome. It is rather surprising that so many seemingly normal American parents send their children out onto the streets and encourage them to spend the evening begging complete strangers to give them sweets.

181

The sympathy America gained after September 11th has now all been squandered.

182

Modern political spin and deceit originated with Josef Goebbels (Hitler's propaganda chief and chief media manipulator) but has been refined in America. Spin and deceit are America's gifts to the modern world. There is a huge difference between the insight and judgement of Sun Tzu (the author of *The Art of War*) and, indeed, Macchiavelli, and the deceit practised on the voters by modern politicians.

183

The Americans (who probably killed more British soldiers than the Iraqis did in the Gulf War) came up with phrases such as 'friendly fire' (we shot our allies by mistake) and 'collateral damage' (we killed some women and children by mistake). They have also given us 'planned obsolescence' and 'conspicuous consumption'. Phrases like this are designed to make the unacceptable appear tolerable.

184

It seems possible that the American spacecraft which burnt to a cinder when attempting to return to earth may have collided with bits of rubbish floating in space. Now, which nation (not content with spoiling the Earth) has been polluting space with debris for the last few decades? (The Americans released pictures from inside the doomed spacecraft at the height of the discussions about whether or not Iraq should be invaded in 2003. Cynics might assume that the Americans were trying to garner sympathy for their country.)

185

Since the September 11th attack on the USA there has been a 70 per cent increase in the sale of guns in America. Before this increase in the number of guns available the statistics showed that 89 Americans (12 of those being children) were killed each day by guns. Even at the old (pre September 11th) rate Americans were killing as many fellow citizens each month as the terrorists managed to kill in the attack on the twin towers.

186

'I do not know of any country where, in general, less independence of mind and genuine freedom of discussion reign than in America.'
ALEXIS DE TOCQUEVILLE (WRITING IN THE 19TH CENTURY)

187

A reassuring, recent survey showed that only 40 per cent of Americans trust their Government.

188

When planning their 2003 war on Iraq the American Government said it had allocated a measly £15 million (equal to around 70p per Iraqi) to international aid agencies to help feed, clothe and house Iraqis suffering as a result of the American bombing. The USA Government also announced that it was prepared to give enough daily rations to feed 3 million people (around 12 per cent of the population) for one whole day. At the same time as this was announced the USA said that it was 'prepared to lend' Turkey a massive £5.4 billion and to give it around £4.5 billion in return for permission to send 62,000 American troops into Iraq from Turkey. A total bribe (sorry, 'aid package') of around £10 billion.

(Part of the deal with Turkey will allow Turkish forces to go into Iraq with American troops to make sure that the Kurds (Turkey's neighbours) do not take control. Since the Americans will not allow the Shiites in Iraq to take control because they would form a fundamentalist bond with Iran, the result will be that Saddam Hussein will be replaced by someone from the Sunni tribe – the same tribe from which Saddam Hussein comes. Nothing will change.

Experts estimate the whole cost of the war to American taxpayers to be in the region of £1,000,000,000,000,000.

In due course the Americans will doubtless boast of their generosity towards the Iraqi people (and expect their undying gratitude).

189

American food companies insist that names such as 'Cheddar', 'Emmenthal' and 'Parmesan' should no longer be applied only to cheeses from specific areas of England, Switzerland or Italy. The Americans claim they are entitled to use those names to describe their own products. The Americans also claim that the word 'champagne' is generic; though this is disputed by winemakers from the Champagne region of France who have established the right to keep the word 'champagne' to describe their own specific product.

190

Golf was invented in Scotland. The Royal and Ancient Golf Club in Scotland has always made the rules for the game of golf. These rules are obeyed in every country in the world except in America. The Americans insist on making their own rules. (Apart from golf the Americans prefer to play games – such as American football and baseball – which aren't played in other countries. They can then always claim to be the best in the world.)

191

Independent speech analysts have alleged that George W. Bush is a sociopath: a hostile, angry and dangerous man. When he speaks of war, death, killing, revenge and retribution Bush does not make mistakes. However, when he speaks of matters which require compassion, kindness and understanding he becomes confused. It is then that he produces the 'Bushisms' for which he is now so famous.

192

When he was a congressman, USA vice president Dick Cheney voted against the Equal Rights Amendment, against a resolution calling for South Africa to release Nelson Mandela from prison and against federal funding for abortions, even in cases of rape or incest. As vice-president of the USA, Dick Cheney is presumably one of Tony Blair's new friends.

193

The American arms industry has grown so big that permanent war (as forecast by George Orwell in his book *1984*) has now become an economic necessity. The arms industry needs a constant supply of new orders in order to stay alive but bullets, bombs, land-mines and missiles tend to have a fairly long shelf life. They don't go 'off' if not used within four weeks. Tanks don't suddenly collapse after nine months of sitting parked on a parade ground. Without regular wars the warehouses soon fill up with bullets, land-mines and missiles. The only solution is, of course, to use up some of the arms so that the arms factories can sell some more. Regular wars provide an excuse for increasing military spending.

The end of the Cold War left many Americans wondering why their Government had to spend so much money on armaments – instead of on providing decent housing, schooling and medical care for the poor. The 'permanent war' now being fought by George W. Bush and his colleagues solves the problem for the arms industry. Carpet bombing Afghanistan and Iraq keeps the bomb-making factories busy. After Iraq the Americans will presumably carpet bomb Korea. And then where next?

194

James Madison said 'It is a universal truth that the loss of liberty at home is to be charged to the provisions against danger, real or pretended, from abroad.' Fear of foreign perils, Madison realised, can easily persuade a freedom-loving people to voluntarily part with liberties they would otherwise consider indispensable.'
WILLIAM J. WATKINS JR, *COMBATTING TERRORISM & LESSONS OF 1798*

195

'Since becoming USA president, George W. Bush has dumped the Kyoto global warming treaty, buried a global agreement to enforce a ban on biological weapons, withdrawn from the 1972 anti ballistic

missile treaty on nuclear arms control and deliberately ignored the long standing Geneva Convention. America is, it seems, on a straight isolationist path and is apparently determined to make up its own rules. The rest of the world has been Bush-whacked.'
READER'S LETTER

196

'I have made good judgements in the past. I have made good judgements in the future.'
GEORGE W. BUSH, PRESIDENT OF THE USA,
GOING FOR THE SCIENCE FICTION FAN VOTE.

197

An American company has been given a patent in basmati rice (by the Americans, of course). The peasants who perfected this variety of rice now cannot use it unless they pay the American company holding the 'worldwide' patent.

Farmers in India have for hundreds of years used the neem plant. It possesses many valuable properties. Because of its value the plant has now been 'discovered' and patented by an American company. It is now too expensive for most ordinary Indians to buy.

Global corporations, mostly American, now own many of the seeds of established crops. Peasants can no longer sow the seeds they save from the plants they grow. They must buy their seeds, every year, from big American seed companies. The peasants can't afford to do this. So the poor people in countries around the world starve to death unless they buy expensive food from American companies.

Because they can't afford to pay the high prices charged, governments and charities have to intervene – using taxpayers' money to help ensure the continued rising profits of the companies concerned.

198

In America, where the drugs war costs $80 billion a year, drug prohibition causes more deaths than drug use. The New York County Lawyers Association once stated that drug prohibition killed at least 7,100 people a year whereas the figures for the same period showed that illegal drug use led to 3,652 deaths a year.

The American drugs war leads to around 750,000 arrests a year but most of those are simply users rather than suppliers. The courts are clogged. On the relatively rare occasions when significant shipments are seized the producers merely replace them. Even the most optimistic drug control officers admit that they seize only around 5 per cent of the drugs entering any country illegally.

The Americans are slowly discovering that laws don't stop people using drugs. However, it shouldn't have taken them so long to find this out. During Prohibition in America in the 1920s the amount of alcohol consumed went up. After prohibition ended the amount of alcohol being produced and consumed fell by fifty per cent. The evidence shows that if drug laws have any effect on people's behaviour it is to encourage them to use more drugs.

199

Shortly after I had published articles about America on my web site www.vernoncoleman.com, the server was hacked into and destroyed. The British police traced the cybervandal to America and asked the FBI to investigate. The FBI did nothing. I wrote to Mr William Farish, American Ambassador to the UK pointing out that my web site had been destroyed by a hacker and that the British police had traced the culprit to an address in the USA. I asked Farish to investigate the fact that although the FBI had been asked for help nothing had been done. 'Does not the American Government take hacking seriously?' I asked. 'Does the American Government have no interest in the future security and viability of the internet?' I received no reply.

The Americans have, of course, insisted that the British police arrest British citizens accused of interfering with American web sites.

200

The internet has no future at all. The combined activities of American censors, an oppressive American Government and American hackers mean that in future the internet (invented by an Englishman) will simply become a vast shopping mall. That's it. That's the brave new world the internet has become.

201

The American government has suppressed research work which took nine years to complete and which verified the link between electrosmog (electromagnetic fields), cerebral illnesses and cancer.

The suppressed report was compiled for the USA government and concluded: 'Even weak electromagnetic fields can impair health [if] their effect exists over a long period. They lead to disturbance of the production of the hormone melatonin, which is known to be an important biochemical link. A deficit in this hormone favours the developing of, for example, breast cancer as well as the developing of degenerative cerebral illnesses such as Parkinson's Disease or Alzheimer's Disease, but also brings on heart problems.'

The suppressed report also confirmed that electromagnetic fields can bring on leukaemia in children.

'In addition,' continued the authors of the report, 'there is an increased risk of developing leukaemia and also brain tumours for adults who are exposed to strong fields due to their professions.'

The assumption is that the electromagnetic fields cause a disturbance in the biochemical function of the cells, or influence certain genes. Both mechanisms can cause permanent damage to the cells. (Genetic engineers use microwaves to open cell membranes and insert alien genes. There must, therefore, be a real risk that the widespread use of mobile phones and microwave ovens etc. may cause widespread and irreversible genetic damage.)

The authors of this suppressed report also pointed out that interactions between electromagnetic rays and the cells of the immune system can favour the beginning of cancer – and that the influence of electromagnetic fields on the reproductive organs may cause disease there too.

The authors of this suppressed study demanded that more research be done and that threshold values for the intensity of electromagnetic fields be lowered to a level that would be exceeded by modern electrical wiring and ordinary household appliances.

The study also suggested that overhead power lines may be a significant threat to human health. The threshold values recommended by this suppressed American report are 5,000 times lower than the internationally recognised threshold values.

It is not difficult to see why the USA government has suppressed this report. If the findings of the report were implemented vast industries would be affected and very few factories, offices or homes would be considered safe.

As an interim measure the authors of this study demanded that what they call the 'permanent radiation bombardment' to which we are all subjected should be reduced step by step. They recommended that all overhead power lines should be removed from residential areas and that houses and schools should no longer be built anywhere near to power lines.

The report was suppressed. None of this action has been taken, either in America or elsewhere.

202

In 1982, America gave the world e.coli 0157:H7. This new bug, a direct consequence of genetic engineering, causes dangerous bleeding in the colon, bowel and kidneys of human patients. The first cases occurred in America but outbreaks have now appeared all over the world. An outbreak in Japan in 1996 affected 9,000. In 1997 an outbreak in Scotland killed 20 people. Thank you, America.

203

'UK Tory leader Iain Duncan Smith was reported to have apologised to American television viewers for the fact that 'a minority' of Britons objected to the way the Americans treated their Muslim prisoners. This

whining 'apology' was as inaccurate as it was contemptible. Millions of
British citizens object to the way the Americans treat their prisoners.'
READER'S LETTER

204

'During the fiasco of an election which made George W. Bush president of the USA, the decision by the largely republican appointed justices not to bother counting all the votes in Florida lest the result hand the election to the other candidate (Mr Gore) didn't seem entirely fair and, indeed, seemed more the sort of thing that would have gone down well in one of those tiny countries Mr Bush has probably never heard of but which his advisers will be encouraging him to bomb to bits in the coming years.

Mr Bush is reputedly as bright as the average Florida voter, and is said to have succeeded in the past by exceeding low expectations. The effect he is likely to have on our health was perhaps best illustrated by the fact that tobacco shares rose when it was announced that the modest handful of political appointees who have hijacked voting rights in the USA decided that he, not the other fellow, should get the big job. That pretty much says it all. We can only hope that indignant Americans will now have the courage to sing 'Hail To The Thief' on ceremonial occasions. And the next time the Americans have the nerve to moan about elections in China, Russia or Cuba we can all blow raspberries at them. If George W. Bush is a democratically elected president then so is Fidel Castro.'

FROM *VERNON COLEMAN'S NEWSLETTER* (SHORTLY AFTER GEORGE
W. BUSH WAS ELECTED PRESIDENT OF THE USA).

205

'(USA Policy) is clearly...motivated by George W. Bush's desire to
please the arms and oil industries.'
NELSON MANDELA

206

A course guide for a women's studies class at an American University asks: 'Is Beethoven's Ninth Symphony a marvel of abstract architecture culminating in a gender-free paean to human solidarity or does it model the process of rape.'

207

A recent survey showed that 51 per cent of American people think that George W. Bush cares more about Big Business than ordinary people. No surprise there. The worrying thing is that 39 per cent of Americans believe that George W. Bush cares more about ordinary people than about Big Business. Surely this must mean that 39 per cent of Americans are certifiable?

208

'Bin Laden is in Afghanistan, in some other country or dead.'
ANNOUNCEMENT MADE AFTER 11TH SEPTEMBER 2001 BY A HIGH
RANKING AMERICAN GOVERNMENT OFFICIAL REASSURING AMERICAN
CITIZENS THAT THEIR GOVERNMENT HAD OSAMA BIN LADEN PRETTY
MUCH PINNED DOWN.

209

America is developing an unmanned bomber which will be able to flatten foreign cities without risking the lives of American pilots.

210

Following examples from America, the EU is redefining terrorism as: 'acts which seriously affect the political, economic or social structures of a country or an organisation governed by public international law.' Obviously any company or political organisation will fall into the category of a definition governed by international law and so, under this new definition anyone leafleting or writing an article criticising a multinational corporation will be a terrorist.

For example, anyone who writes an article opposing genetic engineering will be a terrorist since what he does will seriously affect the economic structure of an organisation governed by public international law. Anyone publicly (or even privately) criticising a political party in power will be a terrorist.

This new legislation is destroying the very last shred of our freedom. It is now illegal to write anything derogatory about vaccines, genetic engineering, meat, the farming industry. It is now illegal for me to give you a list of chemicals which may cause cancer. It is now illegal for me to list the possible side effects which may be associated with a prescription drug.

211

I suspect that a few people in the world will welcome a war on Iraq more enthusiastically than Osama bin Laden. By bombing Iraq the Americans will unite the Muslim world and give bin Laden's campaign a huge boost. Is it possible that George W. Bush and his cronies could possibly be even more stupid than they seem?

212

'American troops have the right at any time to cross into Pakistan on counter terrorism operations.'
AMERICAN MILITARY OFFICIAL, AFTER AN AMERICAN
BOMBING RAID ON A RELIGIOUS SCHOOL IN PAKISTAN IN 2003.

213

'Naturally, the common people don't want war; neither in Russia, nor in England, nor for that matter in Germany. That is understood. But, after all,

*it is the leaders of the country who determine the policy and it is always a
simple matter to drag the people along, whether it is a democracy or a fascist
dictatorship, or a parliament, or a communist dictatorship. Voice or no voice
the people can always be brought to the bidding of the leaders. That is easy.
All you have to do is tell them they are being attacked and denounce the
peacemakers for lack of patriotism and exposing the country to danger; it
works the same in any country.'*
HERMANN GOERING, HITLER'S NO 2, SPEAKING BEFORE BEING
SENTENCED TO DEATH AT THE NUREMBURG TRIALS AND GIVING ADVICE
OBVIOUSLY USED BY GEORGE W. BUSH AND TONY BLAIR.

214

*'We have tried in this country to impose many things from above. Nothing
ever comes of this. What we must do is involve people in the process of
government and the people will at once put everyone in their right place.'*
MIKHAIL GORBACHEV, EX PRESIDENT USSR, WHO HAD A MUCH
BETTER GRASP OF THE PRINCIPLE OF DEMOCRACY THAN EITHER
GEORGE W. BUSH OR TONY BLAIR.

215

The American 'defence' budget (it would be more accurately described as a war budget) is around $400 billion a year. This is close
to the combined Gross Domestic Product of the whole of Africa.

216

It is becoming clear that American isolationism is greatly responsible for much of its current pain. The CIA, FBI and American state
department are desperately appealing for people who can speak
and write Arabic to come forward to help them decipher documents and communicate with their new enemies. In the book *Holy
War, Inc: Inside the Secret World of Osama bin Laden* Peter L. Bergen
quotes a CIA officer as saying: 'The CIA probably does not have a

single truly qualified Arabic speaking officer of Middle Eastern background who can play a believable Muslim fundamentalist and who would volunteer to spend years of his life with shitty food and no women in the mountains of Afghanistan...Most case officers live in the suburbs of Virginia.'

217

Whatever else you may say about it, it is difficult not to agree that the terrible attack on America in 2001 was well organised and extremely effective. The American response has been vindictive and vengeful but it has also been an indiscriminate shambles.

218

'The failure to take on Saddam after what the president said would produce such a collapse of confidence in the president that it would set back the war on terrorism.'

RICHARD PERLE, CHAIRMAN OF THE AMERICAN DEFENCE ADVISORY BOARD AND ONE OF THE ARCHITECTS OF THE 2003 IRAQ WAR, EXPLAINING WHY BUSH HAD TO GO TO WAR, REGARDLESS OF THE VIEWS OF THE UNITED NATIONS OR THE FINDINGS OF THE WEAPONS INSPECTORS. PERLE IS APPARENTLY KNOWN BY SOME AS THE AMERICAN 'PRINCE OF DARKNESS'.

219

On September 11th, the very day that New York and Washington were attacked, the American government announced that it was still not going to stop the IRA raising money in the USA. On the very same day that it declared war on countries supporting terrorists the American Government announced that it would continue to support the IRA, whose bombing campaigns have terrorised and killed thousands in the UK.

Most British newspapers were so full of reports of the wicked attacks in the USA that they did not report this cruel, ruthless and extreme example of political hypocrisy.

220

'Some wars are justified. America's interference in Yugoslavia and its wars in Afghanistan and Iraq are not justified. What is the difference between unjustified war and terrorism?'
READER'S LETTER

221

'There are an estimated 19 million evangelical Christians in the USA. Many voted for George W. Bush who is a born-again Christian. It is said that his fellow warmonger, Tony Blair, is also a committed Christian. If these men are Christians then give me atheists any day.'
READER'S LETTER

222

Families of the Americans who died on September the 11th 2001 are now suing for $1 trillion. Lawsuits started within hours of the planes hitting the twin towers. Everyone who could possibly be considered culpable in any way seems to have received a writ or two. It was, of course, in America that a woman sued a burger bar after she spilt hot coffee on herself.

223

A black American who pretended to be golfer Tiger Woods and used a fake driving licence and credit cards to purchase a TV set and a second-hand car was sentenced to spend 'two hundred years to life' in prison.

224

'And so, in my State of the – my State of the Union – or state – my speech to the nation, whatever you want to call it, speech to the nation – I asked Americans to give 4,000 years – 4,000 hours over the next – the rest of your life – of service to America.'

THE INCOHERENT GEORGE W. BUSH, PRESIDENT OF AMERICA AND ALLEGEDLY THE MOST POWERFUL MAN IN THE WORLD, TRYING (AND FAILING) TO EXPLAIN HIS COMMUNITY SERVICE INITIATIVE TO THE AMERICAN PEOPLE.

225

The George W. Bush administration imposed a 30 per cent tariff on many imported steel products. This means that the USA Government is subsidising each job in the American steel industry to the tune of $600,000 a year.

226

Terrorists attacked the USA because they dislike its policies. By allying itself so closely with the USA's biased and belligerent attitude towards the Middle East the UK has also made itself a terrorist target. If the UK is attacked will the USA help? Judging by what happened in World War II UK citizens will have to wait a long time and pay a very high price.

227

It cannot be said too often that it is the Americans who steadfastly oppose efforts to ban landmines.

228

Most bits of the American media are now owned by a few conglomerates. In 2002 just nine huge companies dominated the USA and global media. These giants spend $125 million a year lobbying and campaigning against ownership restrictions. In return, the American media rarely, if ever, investigate serious issues – concentrating instead on show business stories and non contentious news events which do not threaten the Government. Critics of the American way are rarely, if ever, given a voice. There isn't much 'freedom of the press' in the USA (There isn't much in the UK either.)

229

'Liberalism denied the state in the name of the individual; fascism reasserts the rights of the state as expressing the real essence of the individual.'
MUSSOLINI, THE MAN WHO INVENTED FASCISM, PROVING FROM BEYOND THE GRAVE THAT GEORGE W. BUSH AND TONY BLAIR ARE FASCISTS.

230

During the build-up to the 2003 Iraqi war the Americans continually tried to find evidence supporting a war. In February 2003, Tony Blair came to their aid with a 19 page document setting out the reasons for supporting America's war against Iraq and detailing Iraq deceptions. However, much of the paper was quickly found to have been cribbed from old magazine articles and a 12 year old student thesis based on Iraqi documents which had been seized in 1991. Junior spin doctors working for Blair had found the thesis and articles on the internet and spun them and beefed them up a bit before claiming them as the result of work done by the Government's intelligence services. (This rather suggests that the Government's intelligence services had nothing of value to offer.) Before the deception was exposed Blair's absurd and dishonestly presented document had been described by General Powell, the USA Secretary of State, as a 'fine paper...which describes in exquisite detail Iraqi deception activities'.

Of course, Powell's own attempt to justify a war wasn't much better.

General Powell claimed that there had been decades of contact between Saddam Hussein and Al Qaeda. His intelligence sources must be poor if he does not realise that Al Qaeda only came into being in 1998. Before that Osama bin Laden had been working for the CIA against the Russians.

Powell produced a dramatic picture of a pilotless Iraqi aircraft capable of spraying poison chemicals. This turned out to be the imaginative work of an artist employed by the Pentagon. America's other evidence proved to be equally feeble.

In more honest and honourable days the British Prime Minister and his responsible Ministers would have resigned after misleading Parliament and the public in such an outrageous manner. Naturally, Tony Blair did not resign.

231

When George W. Bush received an honorary degree by Yale University dozens of professors boycotted the ceremony.

232

The USA is planning to sell off the 'freehold' to radio and TV frequencies. Instead of these frequencies being controlled by the Government (on behalf of the people) they will be sold, in perpetuity, to the highest bidder.

233

The latest figures suggest that the number who died in the awful attacks of September 11th was less than half the original estimate of 6,000. Naturally, the American and British Governments kept quiet about this. A reduction in the number of deaths does not serve their purpose.

234

'The future will be a better tomorrow.'
GEORGE W. BUSH, PRESIDENT OF THE USA, PRESUMABLY NOT TOO CONCERNED WITH THE DAY AFTER TOMORROW.

235

Coronary by-pass operations are immensely popular among heart surgeons (and extremely profitable) but a major study conducted in Europe showed that many patients who don't have surgery live longer than those who do.

In one year in the 1990s, American surgeons performed 350,000 coronary by-pass operations and charged $14 billion for them. Are American surgeons too keen to operate? Figures show that 61 in every 100,000 Americans have a coronary by-pass operation each year. In Britain only about 6 in every 100,000 have the same operation. In Japan 1 in 100,000 patients will have a coronary by-pass operation.

When one researcher studied 300 patients who had had bypass operations at several hospitals in California he discovered that 14 per cent of the patients would have thrived as well without surgery as with it while another 30 per cent were borderline.

An effective programme to treat heart disease without drugs or surgery was devised by a Dr Dean Ornish but when Dr Ornish wanted to test his ideas neither the American government nor the American Heart Association would help fund the research.

It isn't just heart surgery which is done unnecessarily. In America 70 per cent of women will have a hysterectomy at some stage in their lives but in Britain only 20 per cent will have the same operation. In America, 20 per cent of babies are born by Caesarian delivery. In England and Wales the figure is 9 per cent and in Japan 8 per cent of confinements end in a Caesarian delivery.

Experts estimate that up to 70 per cent of hysterectomies and around 50 per cent of lower back disc operations done in the USA are probably unnecessary.

In America the death toll from unnecessary surgery has been estimated to be as high as 80,000 patients per year. Put another way, greedy doctors callously kill 80,000 Americans every year.

236

Everyone assumes that Osama bin Laden is as guilty as the Americans say he is of the September 11th attack, even though the Americans don't seem to have produced anything other than opinions and vague circumstantial evidence, and given the Americans record at making wrong assumptions in this sort of situation this is rather worrying.

Has anyone asked Mr bin Laden what he wants? Has anyone thought of negotiation? Diplomacy? Peace process? No. America has been offended and so the rest of the world must suffer. Remember: America has suffered one terrorist attack. (What country hasn't?). No one has declared war on America.

237

'America − a country which has leapt from barbarism to decadence without touching civilisation.'
JOHN O'HARA

238

'He sits on 10 per cent of the world's oil reserves. He has enormous wealth generated by that. And, left to his own devices, it's the judgement of many that he will soon acquire nuclear weapons,' said USA vice president Dick Cheney explaining America's desire to topple Saddam Hussein and take over Iraq.

The USA has more nuclear weapons than any other country and is, of course, the only country in the world to have used nuclear weapons.

CHINA, RUSSIA, INDIA, ISRAEL AND PAKISTAN ALL HAVE NUCLEAR WEAPONS. NONE OF THEM HAVE EVER USED THEM.

BUSH DECIDED TO BOMB IRAQ BECAUSE IT 'MIGHT' DEVELOP WEAPONS OF MASS DESTRUCTION (AND BE A THREAT TO WORLD PEACE). IS HE ALSO GOING TO BOMB INDIA, PAKISTAN AND ISRAEL – ALL OF WHICH NATIONS COULD BE DESCRIBED AS POSING A SIMILAR OR GREATER THREAT TO WORLD PEACE? WHERE AND WHEN WILL THE BOMBING STOP? THE MOST AGGRESSIVE NATION IN THE WORLD IS AMERICA.

239

The International Monetary Fund and the North American Free Trade Agreement (NAFTA) are successfully managing to put small farmers out of business – both in America and Canada and in Mexico.

Huge farming corporations use cheap labour in Mexico (where they can also use banned chemicals and pesticides which help increase production) and then use NAFTA rules to enable them to import the produce into the USA.

The results are that small farmers in all three countries suffer, consumers eat food which is potentially dangerous and international corporations make bigger profits.

240

The Americans always like to claim that they have invented everything. In fact they have invented relatively little – preferring instead to steal from other countries. Over the last 250 years, Englishmen and Englishwomen have been responsible for nearly four out of every five major inventions, discoveries and new technologies. Moreover, Japanese research shows that more than half of the world's most useful inventions since 1945 were made by Englishmen and Englishwomen. (Just for comparison, Americans have contributed under one fifth of the world's useful inventions since 1945.)

The Americans often claim to have invented fast food. But not even that is their invention. Just about every country in the world has its own version of fast food. (In Britain the traditional fast food is 'fish and chips' – far more nutritious than a 'harmburger'.)

241

The Americans often seem to enjoy ignoring or besmirching anything English, while at the same time aggrandising themselves. Their cultural contribution to the world is remarkably small and it is difficult to avoid the conclusion that their eagerness to belittle the English is a result of a combination of jealousy and a feeling of general inadequacy.

242

Thanks to America, you're not as free as you were. (And things are getting worse).

243

The intrusive habit of adding fluoride to water supplies began in America in 1945 and is now common throughout the so-called developed world.

When politicians were told that tooth decay was more prevalent in areas where fluoride was not a natural constituent of local water supplies they decided to reduce health costs by artificially adding fluoride to water supplies.

There are several reasons why you should disapprove of adding fluoride to drinking water.

First, putting fluoride into drinking water is a dangerous business. The amount of fluoride that can safely be added to drinking water has to be judged very carefully. Too much fluoride can cause bone disorders and cancer. Way back in 1986 the World Health Organisation published a report expressing concern about the incidence of problems caused by excessive fluoride in drinking water supplies. Even if you feel that you can trust the scientists to get their sums right when calculating how much fluoride should be added (and don't forget that no one at the water company has the faintest idea how much water *you* are going to drink) there is a very real danger that a water company employee may add the wrong amount of fluoride to your drinking water. Do not accept bland reassurances from your water company. They will undoubtedly assure you that they have checking systems which make such a mishap quite impossible. Ignore these reassurances. If your water company is adding chemicals such as fluoride to your drinking water there is a not insignificant chance that one day an employee will make a mistake and poison you. And unless the error is so terrible that it immediately causes obvious ill health there is a very good chance that you will never even know that a mistake has been made.

Second, many people are allergic to chemicals such as fluoride and may be made ill by drinking water which has had fluoride added to it.

Third, there has to be a real risk that the fluoride which is added to drinking water may interact in some unpredictable way with any one of the many other chemicals which these days occur naturally in many drinking water supplies. The water which comes out of your tap is already likely to contain nitrates (which will have accumulated because of the widespread use of fertilizers in the countryside), chlorine and aluminium sulphate (often added deliberately by water companies) and lead and copper from the pipes which are used to bring water into your home. Whenever chemicals exist in solution together there are chemical reactions. I don't know what all these chemicals will do when they meet one another. And I don't think anyone else really knows either.

Adding chemicals to drinking water is a gross intrusion. Fluoride is merely the beginning and if we allow the scientists, politicians and water companies to get away with this there is no knowing where it will all end. One scientist has already suggested that drinking water should have antibiotics added to it (arguing that this would reduce the risk of infection and so reduce health costs). A second serious suggestion has been that contraceptives be added to drinking water in order to reduce the birth rate. And another suggestion has been that tranquillisers be added to drinking water in order to reduce anxiety levels (and, presumably, keep the voters quiet). It is, of course, already commonplace for farmers to add hormones, antibiotics and tranquillisers to the water (and feed) which they supply to their animals.

244

The dictionary defines terrorism as: 'the use of violence and intimidation for political purposes.' Those who support George W. Bush are supporting terrorism.

245

'...the USA approach is to allow marketing without prior testing of G.M. soods that are deemed to be 'substantially equivalent' to the non-GM variety. Many scientists question whether this is a sufficient basis for regulatory approval.'
PASCAL LAMY, EU TRADE COMMISSIONER

246

The Americans have claimed that Iraq's support for the Palestinian Hamas organisation is proof that Saddam Hussein supports 'terror'. The Americans, on the other hand, see nothing wrong in their support of Israel and its illegal occupation of Palestinian land. Nor do they see anything wrong in their support of the IRA.

247

Colombia is the USA's third largest recipient of foreign aid (behind Israel and Egypt). The USA Congress gives huge amounts of financial support (billions of dollars) to the Colombian Government and also trains the Colombian military. For years now, Colombian citizens have been the victims of human rights atrocities committed by USA trained soldiers. Since 1986, around 4,000 trade unionists have been murdered in Colombia. Since 2001, Colombian aircraft, sponsored by the USA, have been spraying toxic herbicides over Colombian fields to kill opium poppy and coca plants. Inevitably, the toxic sprays have also killed food crops and contaminated water. They have damaged the health of the farmers too.

248

'I found the whole campaign experience inebriating.'
GEORGE W. BUSH, PRESIDENT OF THE USA AND A MAN KNOWN TO
HAVE ENJOYED A DRINK IN HIS TIME.

249

After 11th September 2001, the American Government employed a former advertising executive to 'sell America' to the world. (I don't think it worked terribly well.)

250

There is very little justice in the USA. The treatment of the former Taliban fighters now held without trial by the American Government is an astonishing infringement of human rights and a breach of the Geneva Convention.

251

To paraphrase Jean Paul Sartre: 'Of course the Americans could bomb Iraq. The real question was: 'Could they *not* bomb Iraq?''

252

'Sometimes I wonder whether the world is being run by smart people who are putting us on, or by imbeciles who really mean it.'
Mark Twain

253

Donald Rumsfield, Chief Hawk and Secretary of Defence in George W. Bush's Administration is a long-time White House employee. He worked there (alongside Dick Cheney) with former USA president Richard Nixon and then as USA president Gerald Ford's Secretary of Defence. Rumsfield, who was at one time Chief Executive Officer of the G. D. Searle drug company, has consistently opposed arms control.

254

The Defence Secretary in the UK has claimed that Britain's Armed Forces are to be reshaped because their future role will be to help America invade 'failed states'.

Who is going to decide which states have failed and need to be invaded?

Aren't you supposed to declare war on a country before invading it? Don't you have to have a good reason? Is the world now being run by social workers?

255

'The Americans are rich (through theft), have a lot of weapons to use up and are mightily annoyed that for the first time in their history citizens were killed on their soil. They want to hit back at anyone.'
READER'S LETTER

256

American political leaders are, they claim, destroying our freedom in order to protect it.

That's the same as saying: 'What a nice vase you have got there. I'll smash it for you so that no one can damage it.'

257

During America's 'humanitarian' war against Yugoslavia the USA dropped over 10,000 tons of depleted uranium on (among others) passenger trains, television studios, occupied office buildings, assorted embassies and refugee convoys. This typically inaccurate American bombing campaign was carried out without the authorisation of the United Nations Security Council or, indeed, the USA Congress. It was, in short, an illegal war which would have been described as terrorism if America had not been responsible.

258

America is not a democracy. At the last presidential election George W. Bush, currently president of the USA, obtained less votes than the other candidate, Al Gore, but was 'given' the Presidency by a system which would have produced cries of 'foul' and 'rigged' in a developing country. Thousands of citizens were disenfranchised in order to ensure that Bush got the Presidency. Al Gore lost the last election (and George W. Bush won it) because five American judges wouldn't allow all the votes in Florida to be counted.

259

When George W. Bush was told that terrorists had attacked America on 11/9 the president appeared to receive the news with a look of panic in his eyes. He spent the next nine hours flying from one air base to another and keeping away from Washington. Later that night he regained his courage, added some Texan belligerence and announced: 'We will get whoever did this.'

260

'The (USA) Government has been seized by a ne'er do well rich boy and his elderly henchmen.'
FROM JACKET COPY OF *STUPID WHITE MEN* BY MICHAEL MOORE

261

'I own a car which was made by an American owned company. I spent ages searching in the manual for details of tyre pressure. I eventually found the information I wanted under the heading 'tire pressure'. What, pray, is a 'tire'?'
READER'S LETTER

262

More than half of all American women who reach the age of 65 will have been widowed at least once.

263

'Either you are with America or you are with the terrorists.'
GEORGE W. BUSH, PRESIDENT OF THE USA, CLASSIFYING THE POPE, THE CATHOLIC CHURCH AND APPROXIMATELY 90 PER CENT OF THE WORLD'S POPULATION AS TERRORISTS.

264

The United Nations Charter only sanctions the use of force in the case of an attack on a member state.

265

A French book called *Bin Laden: La Verite Interdite,* written by French intelligence analysts Jean-Charles Brisard and Guillaume Dasquie, claims that the Bush Administration in the USA halted investigations into terrorist activities related to the bin Laden family and began planning for a war against Afghanistan before the events of 11.9.2001.

The two authors allege that, under the influence of American oil companies, George W. Bush and friends stopped investigations into terrorism while bargaining with the Taliban in Afghanistan to give them Osama bin Laden in return for political recognition and economic aid. It is claimed that the USA Government wanted to deal with the Taliban (rather than overthrow it) so that it could gain access to the oil and gas reserves in Central Asia and build an oil pipeline.

It is also alleged that the USA had, as an alternative, been planning to invade Afghanistan at least three years before the 11/9 attack. The attack of the 11th September was merely a good excuse for the war and the invasion.

It has been reported that the USA Government told the Indian Government in June 2001 that there would be an invasion of Afghanistan in October 2001. Defence analysts had reported the planned invasion as early as March 2001.

All this supports the widely discussed allegation that the American Government knew about the 11/9 attack but did nothing to stop it.

266

'If Blair does not realise that the Americans are driven by oil and money then he must be a complete fool. Everyone I've spoken to think the man is either crooked or stupid. He could, I suppose, be both.'
READER'S LETTER

267

The weather in Western Europe UK will continue to get more unpredictable – and more hazardous in winter – as global warming continues. In 2002, the weather in England and Wales was the wettest since meteorological records began in 1766 – and things are going to get wetter.

As the world gets warmer the atmosphere is capable of holding more moisture and things are going to get worse – particularly now that president George W. Bush of the USA has rejected the Kyoto Protocol for cutting carbon emissions.

Areas like the plains around the Rhine and much of southern Britain are likely to be flooded every year.

268

Number 10 Downing Street was bombed when John Major was Prime Minister. There was glass and debris everywhere. Major is reported to have looked around and said: 'I suppose we will have to find somewhere else to finish the meeting.'

The Americans would have hidden under the table for a week, and emerged only to call in their lawyers so that they could sue for damages.

269

Australia's first immigrants were Britain's rejects: the tough, the feisty, the imaginative and the devious. Modern America, on the other hand, was started off by a bunch of puritans. It shows.

270

'The United Nations Security Council has given the USA peacekeeping forces immunity from the International War Crimes Tribunal. Forces from other countries do not have that immunity. Given their propensity for shooting or

bombing the wrong people the Americans will probably need their immunity.
The Americans – who won this special treatment by blackmailing the
international community – will doubtless continue to wonder why they are
hated by the rest of the world.'
READER'S LETTER

271

Nearly six million American families are homeless. In New York there are an estimated 30,000 people living in shelters. Thousands more live on the street. In Chicago there are an estimated 50,000 people living on the streets. Housing for middle class families is now becoming as scarce as housing was for low income families a decade ago. (Housing for low income families is now virtually impossible to find in much of America.)

272

America's decision to use nuclear weapons against nations it does not like (and which may not even have nuclear capability let alone have used it or threatened to use it) was virtually ignored by British politicians but is surely one of the most significant post World War II decisions.

273

'Barrifs and terriers.'
GEORGE W. BUSH TRYING TO GET HIS BRAIN AROUND
THE COMPLEX SUBJECT OF TARIFFS AND BARRIERS.

274

'The Americans paid Milosovic's successors £50,000,000 to have
Milosovic arrested. The West needs a 'baddie' to excuse their activities in

that part of the world, but Milosovic is no worse than Blair and certainly no
more of a threat to innocent people than the awful Bush.'
Reader's letter

275

Over two million Americans with severe mental health disorders receive no treatment whatsoever. Many end up homeless or in prison.

One significant reason for this is that politically correct Americans have insisted that long-stay mental hospitals be closed down. As a result countless thousands of long-stay patients, unable to earn their own living or even look after themselves, have been thrown out onto the streets to fend for themselves.

276

'The ghastly Blair is clearly desperate to be remembered. He will be
remembered; but in the same breath as Hitler, Mussolini and other fascists.'
Reader's letter

277

Americans are committed meat eaters. Americans now eat the flesh of one million animals per hour. Every day of the week. Every week of the month. Every month of the year.

278

'My government is the world's leading purveyor of violence.'
Dr Martin Luther King

279

In the presidential election which put him in power George W. Bush received votes from just 24 per cent of citizens eligible to vote.

280

'If a person, company or nation (except the USA) spends too much it has to cut back. With nations it means raising taxes or cutting benefits or subsidies. The USA doesn't have to do that, as its current account balance is financed by the world. That deficit is gigantic and grows daily. USA 'growth' is thus artificial, subsidised by the world. The Teflon USA is protected by the fiat $ system. The USA can run debt to the moon while the rest of the world pays the bill. The IMF never imposes anything on the USA as the USA 'owns' the IMF. That's the USA 'success story'.'
CHEVALIER HARRY D. SCHULTZ, PUBLISHER AND WRITER OF THE *HSL NEWSLETTER.*

281

More than 300 experts who sit on 18 advisory committees are paid to advise the USA government on the safety and effectiveness of medicines. Over half of these experts have a direct financial interest in the drug or subject they have been hired to evaluate. Some of the experts receive consulting fees, others have research grants from the companies they are supposed to be investigating and the remainder have shares or stock options.

282

'It is becoming politically suicidal for any foreign leader to be forthrightly pro-American.'
NEWSWEEK

283

'I know how hard it is for you to put food on your family.'
George W. Bush, president of the USA, showing sympathy for
messy eaters.

284

*'We hold these truths to be self evident, that all men are created equal, that
they are endowed by their Creator with certain unalienable Rights, that
among these are Life, Liberty and the pursuit of happiness. That to secure
these Rights, Governments are instituted among Men, deriving their just
powers from the consent of the governed, that whenever any Form of
Government becomes destructive of these ends, it is the Right of the People to
abolish it and institute a new Government, laying its foundations on such
principles and organising its powers in such form as to them shall seem most
likely to effect their Safety and Happiness.'*
The American Declaration of Independence
(formalising and legalising the prospect of revolution).

285

American War movies always show Americans to be the heroes –
even if this means changing the truth. In film after film, British
troops are shown as incompetent or criminal while American troops
are always given all the credit for every success. An innocent ob-
server watching modern American films would assume that only
America was involved in fighting the Germans, the Japanese and
the Italians in the Second World War.

In a film about the capture of the German Enigma code machine the Allied cause has been turned into an American event. In
reality the Enigma code machine was captured by British sailors
before America entered the war. In the film the event involved only
Americans.

It is hardly surprising that American people seriously believe
that their involvement in World War II was crucial and that 'the

Europeans should be grateful to America for having given them their freedom'.

Americans commonly claim that the USA won World War II – and saved England from Nazi rule. This is a myth. The USA did not come to Europe's help in World War II.

During the Second World War, Roosevelt's response to Churchill's request for help was to agree to give Britain fifty old and pretty useless destroyers to help with the war effort. In return, Churchill had to hand over a ring of valuable British bases. When Churchill asked for more help the USA demanded all the UK's gold, as much money as the UK could borrow and insisted that all available public and private assets be sold. Britain had to buy the arms supplied by America. The Americans demanded entry to Britain's export markets and Britain had to hand over details of numerous new British inventions (including the jet engine). These were goodwill gifts which the USA demanded not in return for helping Britain in the war against Hitler (they didn't) but simply to agree to sell arms to Britain.

Roosevelt and the USA did nothing to help Britain until Germany made the mistake of declaring war on the USA.

America's post war economic success was and is built upon the exploitation of Britain during the earliest war years. That is a fact which we should never forget.

If it had been left to the USA Hitler would have become Supreme Commander of the entire world.

After Pearl Harbour, Churchill was terrified that the Americans would enter the war but would concentrate all their war effort on the Pacific.

However, Europe was saved when Hitler and Mussolini declared war on the USA on December 11th 1941. It was only then that America was forced into the war. It was Russia, led by Stalin, which helped Britain most (not the USA). The Russian army destroyed far more of the German army than the Americans did.

The American war effort (such as it was) was littered with strategic and tactical incompetencies, jealousies and conceits. Britain ended the Second World War ruined, both industrially and economically. Britain had massive war debts, devastated cities and an industry in ruins. She was relegated to the second rank scientifically and had a vast percentage of her brightest, strongest and toughest young men buried in graves throughout Europe.

It is obscene, and an insult to the memory of those Britons who died in World War II, that British leaders should now claim that the UK has a special relationship with the USA because of World War II.

286

'This is Preservation Month. I appreciate Preservation. It's what you do when you run for president. You gotta Preserve.'
GEORGE W. BUSH, THE AMERICAN PRESIDENT, ATTENDING A CELEBRATION FOR 'PERSEVERANCE MONTH' AT A SCHOOL CEREMONY BUT, SADLY, HAVING MISUNDERSTOOD THE PURPOSE OF THE EVENT.

287

After the American Government introduced laws enabling it to put people in prison without trial (simply on suspicion of terrorism) the British Government followed suit.

The number of people now classified as terrorists grows daily. For example, animal lovers who protest about the abuse of animals are officially classified as terrorists. Carry a placard or write a letter protesting about vivisection or hunting and you are a terrorist.

288

America uses economic force to pressurise the rest of the world into accepting steroid enriched meat and genetically engineered food. Countries which do not accept these products are likely to find themselves at the wrong end of arbitrarily appointed American sanctions. ('If you won't buy our hormone enriched beef we won't buy your umbrellas, whisky, cars or shoes.')

289

America's war against terrorism, and the decision to attack Iraq (and claim their oil) is not a consequence of September 11th. The September 11th attack was no more than an excuse for a long-planned event – plus a whole raft of belligerent anti-freedom activities.

290

'Mr Blair is like a front-seat passenger in a car driven at speed into a fog by a headstrong driver who ignores all pleas to slow down and roars past all warning signs. We, the British people, are the hapless passengers in the back.'
CORRELLI BARNETT, THE AUTHOR OF *THE AUDIT OF WAR*

291

'The Americans are rich not because they work harder than everyone else but because they pollute the world and don't clean up after themselves, they steal other people's property (such as seeds), they bully other countries into accepting technology which isn't wanted and isn't safe (such as genetic engineering and the use of growth hormones in cattle) and they take advantage of poorer countries (constantly finding new ways to transfer wealth from starving people in impoverished countries to themselves). The Americans are ruthless, cruel and hypocritical.'
READER'S LETTER

292

One of the reasons why the UK stock market fell so rapidly in 2002 was the fact that Americans were dumping shares in UK companies. Although the UK stock market accounts for only 8.4 per cent of the world's stock market, the UK market accounted for 33.6 per cent of American net selling in just one month. The British stock market may prove more stable, and less dependent on Wall Street, now that fewer Americans have holdings in the UK.

293

America has turned vast quantities of South American rainforest into grassland so that cattle can be raised to provide obese Americans with 'harmburgers'.

294

'Captured soldiers should be kindly treated and kept.'
SUN TZU, *THE ART OF WAR*

295

'I am appalled by the number of recent American films which have misrepresented the part played by American troops in World War II. Surely writers and makers of films have a responsibility to tell the truth if the event they are representing is a genuine one, which involved real people and is of historical importance? The American appetite for self-aggrandisement seems endless.'
READER'S LETTER

296

Travelling through Europe these days it is impossible to avoid Americans. And, sadly, the experiences are not usually pleasant ones. I sat in one cafe and watched in horrified embarrassment as a large party of Americans trooped in and, although they were not customers, demanded to be allowed to use the toilets. The waiter kindly pointed them in the right direction. Ten minutes later they all left without so much as a word of thanks.

On a train I shared a carriage with an American family who turned what should have been a pleasant journey into a nightmare. Four of them spread their bodies and luggage over a dozen seats and then proceeded to make incessant demands of the hard working staff. Not once did they say 'please' or 'thank you'.

Other travellers I have spoken to confirm that they have endured similarly embarrassing incidents as marauding armies of arrogant, aggressive and demanding Americans swagger around the world as though they own it.

All this is made worse by the fact that knowledgeable citizens around the rest of the world know that American wealth is subsidised by the way that the American government and American companies abuse the environment and, indeed, whole countries, for the sake of profit.

297

'George W. Bush and Tony Blair should surely be tried before a war crimes tribunal. These guys make Milosovic look like a humanitarian.'
READER'S LETTER

298

American tobacco companies spike their cigarettes with chemicals in order to make them more addictive. They then market their cigarettes to children in developing countries who become addicts and lifelong profit machines.

299

'General. I can't name the general. General.'
GEORGE W. BUSH ASKED TO NAME THE LEADER OF PAKISTAN BUT GETTING
HALF A POINT FOR BEING ABLE TO IDENTIFY A MILITARY RANK.

300

The USA is the only country in the world to have ever used nuclear weapons but it imposes crippling sanctions on countries (other than Israel) which now develop them. The USA forces other countries to abandon their own nuclear weapons programmes while continuing with the design, production and stockpiling of new nuclear weapons of its own. The American Government, which has now confirmed that it is dedicated to 'endless war' seems addicted to military activity.

301

In an attempt to clean up problems in the running of American corporations (and, in particular, accounting dishonesties among American companies which have led to melt-down in the world's financial markets) George W. Bush signed an act which requires all companies (whether American or not) to obey specific American regulations. Some of these new laws conflict with laws in other countries.

The original problems were created because too many American companies were run dishonestly but with typical American arrogance George W. Bush is attempting to impose new American law on honest companies based in other countries.

302

'I used to regard Americans as simply rather brash − like overweight teenagers with too much pocket money. No more. These days I see Americans as simply arrogant and aggressive.'
READER'S LETTER

303

Why do the Americans need to keep such enormous stocks of military quality anthrax?

304

One of Osama bin Laden's aims in attacking America in September 2001 was to provoke a war between Christians and Muslims. He wanted a culture clash. The Americans, through aggression and stupidity, seem determined to give him the war he wants. The Americans believe they will win. They won't. They will be humiliated in a war which will make the Vietnam War look like a schoolyard scuffle. If America or Israel use nuclear weapons against Iraq we will be heading straight for Armageddon.

305

There have been numerous allegations of links between the Bush family and Osama bin Laden. Bush is alleged to have made serious money with a company financed by a brother of Osama bin Laden. And it is widely known that both the Bush family and the bin Ladens had stakes in the Carlyle Group, a private investment firm which has large USA defence and communications contracts. (Tony Blair's Labour Government sold the UK Ministry of Defence research laboratories to the Carlyle Group.)

306

When France and Germany opposed America's war on Iraq, many Americans accused both countries of ingratitude. France and Germany were both supposed to be grateful for the help the Americans gave them in the Second World War.

This accusation, which seems to ignore the fact that France and Germany were fighting on opposite sides and that even if one country ought to be grateful for American intervention it is difficult to see why both should be, illustrates the depth of ignorance in the USA about what exactly happened in the Second World War.

Countries don't often act out of kindness to their neighbours. Most nations generally act out of self-interest and America always does.

Remember: America entered the Second World War because it had no choice. Germany declared war on an America which, even after Pearl Harbour, was still sitting on the fence waiting to see how things would go. (The American president had consistently refused Churchill's requests for help and had, instead, taken full advantage of Britain's weak bargaining position to make a good deal of money out of the United Kingdom.)

Americans often point to the Marshall Plan as an example of their generosity. But the Marshall Plan was conceived and executed in America's best interests. Those Americans who believe otherwise should check their Government's own records. They will then discover that the USA introduced the Marshall Plan because it feared that without a European recovery the USA itself would be plunged into a depression.

The Americans claim that they saved us from the Soviet Union after the Second World War. But the Soviet Union was never a serious threat and, indeed, America did just as much (if not more) sabre rattling as the Russians.

In 1953, after Stalin died, Churchill was keen to work towards a peace with the Russians. After all, far more Russians than Germans had died fighting the German army. But the Americans weren't interested in peace with the Russians. The Cold War was created largely because America feared that the Russians were intent on spreading their 'Union' widely into Eastern Europe and thereafter into the rest of the world. This was a typical piece of American paranoia. The Russians were simply intent on building something of a barrier between themselves and the Germans. They had, after all, been invaded by the Germans twice in the first half of the twentieth century. The real truth is that the Americans didn't save us from the Cold War. They helped create it and then they dragged us into it as 'allies' to cover their backs

307

'I feel impotent, angry and ashamed of my country. It is a terrible feeling. I now know what it must have felt like to be an honest, honourable German in 1939. How can I disassociate myself from Bush — a president who purports to represent me to the world but who,

*I believe, deserves to be tried as a war criminal? I am investigating
ways to abandon my nationality but it isn't easy.'*
AMERICAN READER'S LETTER

308

Organic farming is proving successful and popular. The consumption of organic food is rising dramatically. Americans buy over $6.5 billion worth of organically grown food each year. More and more Americans are, it seems, voting against big business and intensively farmed crops and for healthier and tastier food.

Now, I don't think anyone (least of all organic farmers) objects to the idea of some sort of federal regulation of organically grown food in America. At the last count there were 44 separate bodies trying to set standards for organic food.

But the American food industry seems to have more control over its government than food industries anywhere else in the world. (American consumers don't even have any way of knowing whether or not the food they buy is, or is not, genetically engineered.)

And the American government has been pressurised by industrial farmers (and by the big drug and chemical companies who want to get into the organic food market) who realise that if the market for genuine organic food continues to grow their own profits will inevitably fall.

Inevitably, perhaps, the American government's plans seem designed more to destroy than to protect the organic food growers.

Real organic farming is labour intensive and works best when operated by small scale farmers operating on a restricted local basis. And so serious plans are afoot to destroy proper organic farming before it develops further and does more damage to the established food 'industry'.

The American Government is introducing new 'standards' for organic farming which are likely to have a dramatic effect on the quality of food worldwide. The proposed new standards for organic food are abysmally low – much lower than existing standards. Astonishingly, farms which use drugs and genetically modified organisms will be entitled to certificates declaring their food to be 'organic'. And it will be possible to keep animals on so-called organic farms in cramped factory style conditions – with no opportunity to get outside.

The American Government will allow the powerful food industry to describe food which has been genetically engineered, irradiated, treated with additives or raised on contaminated sewage sludge as 'organic'. And they will allow farmers to describe as 'organic' any livestock which has been housed in batteries, given drugs or fed with the unwanted parts of other animals.

In America there will, in short, soon be no real difference between food described as 'organic' and other 'junk' food.

In order to prevent genuine organic farmers calling their produce something else the USA Government is making it illegal to set standards higher than the ones that it defines. This will effectively make it illegal for farmers to produce and sell good quality food.

To begin with these absurd new regulations will operate only in the USA. But it will not be long before American manufacturers put pressure on their government to force the rest of the world to accept the American definition of 'organic food'.

It is this process which has already seen the European Union force unwilling consumers in all member countries to accept beef and milk contaminated with growth hormones.

309

American activities in Bosnia were reprehensible. The Americans invariably sail under false colours and this war was no exception. Under the guise of ousting Milosevic and 'protecting' people under threat, the Americans were busy establishing for themselves (what they thought would be) a strong foothold in a part of the world which they now regard as having strategic importance.

The Americans (rather naively) hoped that by supporting extreme Islamic fundamentalists (and, for example, creating a fundamentalist Muslim state in the Balkans) they would improve their relationship with oil producing states, be forgiven for their extremist Zionist policies and their involvements on Saudi territory, and justify the enlargement of NATO and the permanent presence of an American army in Europe.

310

Early in his Presidency George W. Bush admitted that global warming exists and is a problem. He also admitted that steps must be taken to reduce emissions (particularly by America, which is the world's worst polluter).

However, the Bush Administration has introduced a new energy plan which will increase (not reduce) the amount of air pollution in the USA.

Bush's new plan will lead to less funding for renewable, clean energy sources (such as wind and solar power) and to increased fossil fuel consumption.

The new George W. Bush plan also lowers upgrade requirements on 60 old power plants (which often emit up to ten times as much sulphur dioxide, carbon dioxide, mercury and other pollutants as new plants). This will lead to increased energy company profits. Coincidentally, the number of respiratory related hospital visits and asthma cases is rising in the USA. (This, however, will lead to increased drug company profits.)

In summary, George W. Bush's new laws will speed up the effects of global warming, seriously damage the environment and adversely affect the health of everyone on the planet.

311

Suggestions have been made that the CIA deliberately incited Iraq to invade Kuwait. The USA presumably wanted an excuse to intervene in the area and 'soften up' Iraq.

312

In cockney rhyming slang Americans (yanks) are known as 'septics'. The rhyme is derived from 'septic tanks'. A 'septic tank' is a container in which sewage is liquefied by bacterial activity.

313

According to *Fortune* magazine 'the universal language of business ... comes from the USA.'

I suppose that's why it's called English.

314

Are Bush and Blair the 21st century axis of evil?

315

USA agents now abduct people they suspect of terrorist activity and send them to countries where torture is legal. Suspects kidnapped by the Americans (who prefer the word 'rendition') are shipped to countries where they can be imprisoned without any specific charges being made against them, where they can be denied legal assistance and where they can be interrogated and tortured. The kidnapped suspects can then be 'rendered' to the USA.

'It allows us to get information from terrorists in a way we can't do on USA soil,' explained an American diplomat who was presumably aware that these kidnappings (a word I prefer) violate human rights laws and extradition laws.

Egypt is one country allegedly used in the 'rendering' process. Coincidentally, Egypt is second only to Israel as a recipient of American foreign aid.

316

For years the world has watched while the Americans have risked world peace by doing everything to help Israel. And yet Israel won't even recognise the word 'Palestine'. British Prime Minister Tony Blair had to grovel to Israel's Prime Minister (a man whom some European jurists want arrested and tried as a war criminal) when Foreign Secretary Jack Straw mentioned the word 'Palestine'.

Independent observers have called for the Israelis to hand over those members of their government who they believe should to be tried for war crimes.

American politicians (and indeed the American people in general) seem unable to recognise that the Palestinians have legitimate complaints. The Israelis are building houses on land that was never meant to be part of Israel. How would the Americans react if Canada suddenly annexed part of the USA?

The quickest way to stop world terrorism is for America to tell Israel to leave the Palestinians alone and to stop falsely claiming Palestinian land.

317

Pornography in the USA is bigger business than baseball, football and basketball put together. It generates more revenues than rock and country music put together. The American porn business is now worth $10-14 billion a year.

318

The Americans are bullies. When they can't get their own way they bully other countries – using financial muscle (economic sanctions) when they think it will help and using force when the financial muscle doesn't work.

319

Bush and Blair claim that replacing Saddam Hussein is a moral act – designed solely to help the people of Iraq. (Although curiously, Tony Blair, who likes to describe himself as a religious man, and who is allegedly planning to become a Catholic, publicly ignored the Pope's plea for no war against Iraq.)

If these two are now concerned with replacing 'undemocratic' leaders when will the wars ever end?

And why aren't the USA and the UK declaring war on themselves? Both have leaders who represent minorities.

Blair repeatedly ignored the large majority of the British electorate who were opposed to a war against Iraq. Can a leader who takes no notice of the people be described as democratic?

320

During the run up to the 2003 Iraq War the Americans, desperate to get the Russian vote for the United Nations security council resolution that would give them the green light to bomb Iraq and grab its oil, promised the Russians that Iraq's outstanding $8 billion debts to Moscow and the Russian oil industry would be honoured in a post-Saddam Hussein Iraq.

In principle, the Americans did not, of course, have any right to make decisions for a post Saddam Hussein regime. In practice, the Russians presumably knew that America would, as conquerors, have control of Iraq's oil and its money. It was, perhaps, a sign of the Americans' desperation that they were prepared to make this deal and, thereby, be rather more obvious about their intentions than they had previously been.

321

The Democratic Republic of Congo (which contains huge stores of diamonds, copper, zinc, coltan, uranium and other minerals and which has been described as 'the richest patch of earth on the planet') has become a target for USA supported neighbours Uganda and Rwanda. Coltan is particularly important since it is used to make mobile phones and is essential in the development of computer chips. The Democratic Republic of Congo holds 80 per cent of the world's known supply of coltan reserves.

For decades American Governments have identified sources of materials in third world countries and have then encouraged American companies to remove those resources for American use. Unfortunately for America, although the Congo has a dictator who was originally more or less installed by the USA, the dictator has gradually limited the amount of minerals he has allowed American companies to remove.

The Americans did not let this stop them. In 1998 the leaders of Rwanda and Uganda (trained by the USA military) invaded the mineral rich parts of the Congo and took over. They naturally allowed American corporations to continue to exploit the rich area.

322

In 2003 the Americans claimed that by opposing their enthusiasm for dropping bombs on Iraq the French and the Germans were endangering NATO.

Once again the Americans needed to study their history books (though preferably not ones written and published in America). NATO was created to deal with the alleged threat posed by the Soviet Union (a threat which existed largely in the minds of the Americans).

By 2003 there was clearly no longer a threat from the Soviet Union and so there was no need for NATO to continue to exist.

The truth is that NATO only existed in 2003 because the well-paid officials who worked for it were determined to keep it alive.

323

I can think of more reasons to want a change of regime in the USA than in Iraq.

324

What happened on September 11th 2001 was terrible. It would have been wonderful if some good could come out of all that violence; if the Americans could have learnt that their policies abroad are creating chaos and unbalancing the world as surely as their environmental abuses are unbalancing nature.

325

When 4,578 instances of execution in the USA were reviewed
was discovered that serious, reversible errors had been made
seven out of every ten capital sentence cases. Unfortunately, it wa
too late for the 70 per cent of prisoners who had been execute
wrongly. Some American prosecutors still won't allow evidence t
be reviewed even when it is clear that a review might lead to a
death sentence being revoked.

A college class at Northwestern University in Illinois recently
studied prisoners on their local death row. They proved that five of
the prisoners were innocent.

326

*'This Administration (of George W. Bush) has turned the patient art of
diplomacy into threats, labelling and name calling of the sort that reflects
quite poorly on the intelligence and sensitivity of our leaders, and which will
have consequences for years to come. Calling heads of state pygmies, labelling
whole countries as evil, denigrating powerful European allies as irrelevant –
these types of crude insensitivities can do our great nation no good.'*
USA SENATOR ROBERT BYRD, SPEAKING IN THE USA SENATE

327

'More and more of our imports come from overseas.'
GEORGE W. BUSH, PRESIDENT OF THE USA, SHOWING THAT HE IS, IF
NOTHING ELSE, CONSISTENT IN HIS IDIOCY.

328

It seems that the formerly massive but now defunct Enron (at one
point allegedly the world's largest company – though very few people had ever heard of it till it went bust and no one seems able to
describe exactly what it did) gave vast amounts of boodle to 71 out

of America's 100 senators. The company also threw money at George W. Bush during his election campaign (around $700,000 seems accurate).

It has been alleged that Enron's extensive interests in the oil industry meant that the company wasn't terribly keen on America sticking to the Kyoto Treaty. It is common knowledge that one of the first actions of George W. Bush when becoming president of the USA was to reject the Kyoto Treaty. Could there possibly be any link between these facts? You can put two and two together just as well as I can. Am I being cynical in concluding that this all seems to suggest that the future of the world was sold for $700,000?

This was a knock down price but Enron got the British Government far cheaper. (It would have been enormously surprising if Britain's most corrupt ever government had not been tainted by the first major scandal of the 21st century.)

329

In 1956 British Prime Minister Anthony Eden joined with France to send troops to Egypt after the Egyptian leader Abdul Gamal Nasser had nationalised the Suez Canal. Eden believed that Nasser posed a threat to the world and had to be eliminated. The military action was a disaster because the Egyptians blocked the canal by sinking ships in it. Britain was humiliated and forced to withdraw because the United States of America refused to back a loan from the International Monetary Fund to help support the collapsing pound.

On every occasion when America has asked Britain for help, Britain has helped. On every occasion when Britain has asked for help from America, America has refused to help.

330

Here is a list of just some of the ways in which America has interfered in other country's business – often starting wars – since the end of the Second World War.

(The Federation of American Scientists has catalogued nearly

two hundred military incursions since 1945 in which the United States of America has been the aggressor.)

This list is just one of many, many reasons why the rest of the world now hates America. If American people want to be loved then they must take tighter control over their Government.

1948 ITALY: America interfered when it looked as though the communists might win power.

1950: KOREA: Ruled by rampant McCarthyism and virulent anti-communism America insisted on getting involved when North Korea invaded South Korea.

1953: IRAN: America supported the overthrow of the government of Iran. The CIA organised street demonstrations. The Ayatollah Khomeini who gained power in 1979 had been on the CIA payroll when he lived in Paris.

1954: GUATEMALA: American trained rebels got rid of the socialist government. The result was a 30 year war and 250,000 deaths. America invaded because land belonging to the United Fruit Company had been nationalised. The company's board of trustees included the then Secretary of State John Foster Dulles and his brother Alan Dulles (who just happened to be boss of the CIA).

1961: CUBA: CIA backed rebels and the Bay of Pigs fiasco made this one sort-of-war the Americans really like to forget. J. F. Kennedy was embarrassed by Fidel Castro and so ordered the assassination of the Cuban president. But the Americans failed in this. In revenge the Americans have used economic sanctions to keep the Cuban people poor.

1963: VIETNAM: America supported South Vietnam. The result? Humiliation for America and the death of approximately 3 million people (a few of them Americans). Most of America now seems to have forgotten the Vietnam War. The rest of the world has not.

1965: DOMINICAN REPUBLIC: America sent 23,000 marines to get rid of a left wing president (even though he wasn't a communist). Why? Why not? More than 3,000 people died.

1968: INDONESIA: General Suharto got to power with the help of the CIA. Suharto proved to be a corrupt dictator. Around 800,000 innocent people died because of American intervention in Indonesia.

1973: CHILE: America wanted to get rid of the Socialist president so they started the coup which resulted in General Pinochet's 17 year reign of terror.

1975: EAST TIMOR: Indonesia invaded East Timor with the support of America. (Although the American Government denied that it had even discussed East Timor with the Indonesian Government the release of previously classified documents show that the Americans gave then president Suharto approval). Around 250,000 innocent people died as a result of American action. According to Amnesty International, East Timor represents one of the worst cases of genocide in the 20th century.

1975: ANGOLA: America got involved in the Angolan civil war and supported right wing groups.

1979: NICARAGUA: America trained 15,000 right wing guerrillas to challenge the Government. When the USA Congress wouldn't pay for any more covert operations the USA president backed the guerrillas with money made by illicitly selling arms to Iran. Here the USA was responsible for the deaths of 30,000 innocent people.

1979: AFGHANISTAN: The USSR invaded. The USA then backed the Islamic 'soldiers of God' (the very people they are currently bombing), trained them and gave them money and arms.

1980: EL SALVADOR: During the 1970s and 1980s the USA Government gave money and arms to the right wing government in El Salvador. The American support helped kill 80,000 innocent people.

1980: ANGOLA: Over a million innocent people were killed in a 15 year war in Angola which was supported by the American Government.

1982: LEBANON: Israel invaded Lebanon and the USA navy began shelling Muslim positions in the Lebanon. Then the American airforce got involved. Then Americans started dying. Then America withdrew. Thousands of people – including many Palestinians – died as a result.

1983: GRENADA: A massive American force invaded Grenada (part of the British Commonwealth) because they claimed a few Americans needed rescuing – though it does not seem clear exactly why or from what they needed rescuing. The Americans then claimed that they needed to invade because of a possible Communist threat. (In fact, a left wing Government had been elected). The invasion was condemned by the UN. The American invasion force was said by some to be more than three times the size of the local population.

1986: Libya: The Americans don't like president Gaddafi because he tried to socialise oil rich Libya. They launched an air attack on Libya in 1986. Gadddafi's small daughter was among the innocent people the Americans killed.

1987: Iraq: After an Iraqi missile was accidentally launched (with the result of 37 American deaths) an American naval ship shot down an Iranian airliner over the Persian Gulf. Nearly 300 people died. The Americans said it was a mistake.

1989: China: USA president Nixon went to China to help Chinese Government hardliners deal with their dissident students. Thousands of freedom seeking students were killed in Tiananmen Square.

1989: Panama: America invaded Panama to get rid of president Noriega (who had previously been associated with the CIA). The Americans claimed that Noriega was a drug dealer but the year after the Americans had moved in the amount of drugs moving through Panama doubled. Over 8,000 innocent Panamanians died as a result of the American invasion.

1991: Iraq: More than 300,000 people died when the Americans tried (and failed) to topple Saddam Hussein in order to protect Kuwaiti oil interests. The Americans bombed the retreating Iraqi army – despite the fact that they were showing white flags of surrender. Since the Americans officially withdrew they have continued to bomb Iraq and economic sanctions have resulted in the deaths of another million innocent men, women and children. For 11 years the USA government has refused to allow aid agencies to provide any humanitarian aid or support in Iraq.

1991: Haiti: The Americans sent in troops after local citizens were foolish enough to elect a liberal priest.

1999: Colombia: America funded a new right wing government (giving them over $1 billion) and arbitrarily sprayed pesticides over local crops – thereby alienating the local citizens and destroying the local economy.

Look down the above list and it is clear that when the Americans invade (or simply bomb) a country they do so purely for their own national interests. They have no interest in the people of the country they are invading (or bombing). And the Americans are so incompetent that they usually manage to kill more innocent people and allies than people they have designated as 'enemies'. They call this: 'losses by friendly fire'.

It is hardly surprising that Martin Luther King said: 'My country is the world's leading purveyor of violence.'

Amazingly, many Americans truly believe that the rest of the world hates America because Americans are rich. The Americans are, it seems, too stupid to realise that if you bomb, kill and maim millions of people around the world you will not be well loved.

The Americans have always been colonialists. That's how they got America in the first place. And the Americans have always had very little sense of shame or of what is right or wrong. They also simply don't seem capable of understanding just how their actions offend others.

Ask the Native Americans.

Modern Americans celebrate the theft of their nation with an annual feast called Thanksgiving. It does not occur to them that this might upset the Native Americans from whom they stole 'their' land in the first place. (It is, therefore, perhaps hardly surprising that they also seem incapable of understanding just how their support of Israel offends the Arabs from whom Israel seems intent to continue stealing land.)

In the wake of the September 11th attack on the USA (a pin prick compared to the damage America has done to other countries) the American Government demanded that the rest of the world offer sympathy and support.

'If you aren't with us you are against us,' they claimed, with astonishing, blood curdling arrogance.

The world hates America because it is now trying to impose its will on everyone else. Colonialism is just not fashionable these days. Until the Americans understand why they are loathed, things will merely get worse.

331

In modern American action films the baddies are almost invariably Arabs. They are, in addition to being evil, invariably ugly and dirty and so incompetent that a single American can kill a hundred of them within seconds without sustaining anything more damaging than mild clothing abrasions.

332

American companies have for years been steadily increasing the use of sweatshops and child labour in Third World countries.

333

When Saddam Hussein used chemical warfare against his own people the Americans did nothing. Why are they now so upset about something that happened years ago, when they didn't give a damn when it happened?

334

Generally speaking, the American media either ignores anti-globalisation protests or marginalises the protestors. Television and newspaper coverage tends to concentrate on the violence (usually the result of unprovoked attacks from security forces) and ignores the arguments.

Protestors claim that they want democratic control over organisations such as the World Trade Organisation, the International Monetary Fund and the World Bank.

However, these claims are simply ignored.

Very few Americans realise that the unelected leaders of these organisations routinely override democratically established laws and regulations in the interests of 'free trade'.

Ironically, more and more ordinary American citizens are now suffering financial hardship as a result of the actions of these organisations.

335

USA Secretary of State and war advocate Colin Powell sat on the boards of computer company AOL and Gulfstream Aerospace (which sells jets to Saudi Arabia) after helping to run the first Iraq war. While Powell was at AOL the company merged with Time Warner (one of the most astonishingly, bizarre and ill-fated consequences of the dot com years). Coincidentally, at the time of the merger, Colin's son Michael was a member of the Federal Communications Commission. He advocated that the merger go through. When AOL merged with Time Warner Colin Powell's shares rocketed in value by approximately £2,500,000.

336

America says it wants to help the world. One billion people in Asia, Africa and Latin America have no access to clean drinking water. Providing those people with water would cost 25 per cent of America's absurd Star Wars military programme.

337

Children in America are more likely to commit suicide with a gun than children anywhere else in the world. And children under 15 are more likely to die from gunfire in the USA than anywhere else on the planet.

338

The USA has still not ratified the UN Convention on the Rights of the Child. Only Somalia has also refused to sign. The Americans won't sign because the Convention prohibits the execution of children under eighteen. The Americans insist on retaining the right to execute children. Not even China executes children.

There are currently nearly 4,000 people on death row in the USA. Nearly 100 of those were children when they committed their crimes.

339

More people are killed and injured in road accidents in the USA than anywhere else (even Belgium).

340

During the Cold War not even America suggested a pre-emptive strike against the Soviet Union – which was known to have far more dangerous weapons than Iraq could possibly possess.

America prefers to pick on countries (such as Iraq) which has no weapons left because they have all been destroyed.

341

There are three times as many rapes in the USA as there are in any other country in the world.

342

'An American friend boasted that the USA has built an aircraft carrier called USA Carl S. Vinson which has a fuel tank capacity of three million gallons – giving it the ability to travel one million miles without re-fuelling. When I asked why would anyone want a ship capable of travelling one million miles without stopping to refuel he could not answer.'
READER'S LETTER

343

'Terrorists are trying to tear down the future because they know America owns it. We still do. It's ours.'
WRITER IN *VANITY FAIR* MAGAZINE

344

The treatment of prisoners in the Cuban camp run by America is an international disgrace. There is (or should be) a difference between justice and revenge. You don't have to be cruel to be strong. The men directly responsible for the atrocities of September 11th are all dead and can no longer be punished. To punish others in a cruel and inhumane way simply as an act of revenge is morally indefensible and politically bizarre. The men in the American prisoner of war camp (and although the Americans deny this, the men clearly are prisoners of war) are being treated without respect or dignity and yet they have been found guilty of nothing.

We don't know who they are or what, if anything, they are supposed to have done. Some are quite probably innocent of anything but being in the wrong place at the wrong time.

If a non oil producing Middle Eastern country captured a large number of Americans and treated them in the way that the Americans are treating their captives there would be an outcry. The fact that the Muslim fighters captured by the Americans are being treated so savagely and without humanity is yet more evidence that the Americans are themselves a simple, racist, primitive people who have not, as a nation, yet earned the right to describe themselves as 'civilised'.

Americans (and their friends) who seem to obtain joy and satisfaction from the way these prisoners are being treated should remember the words of Thomas Jefferson.

Back in 1779 he wrote: 'Is an enemy so execrable that, though in captivity, his wishes and comforts are to be disregarded and even crossed? I think not. It is for the benefit of mankind to mitigate the horrors of war as much as possible.' No country can call itself civilised when it treats captured prisoners with torture, starvation and brainwashing. The means and the end must be in harmony.

Soldiers and leaders who ignored the Geneva Convention during World War II were tried as war criminals. Which nations will now have the courage to try Bush, Rumsfield and their thuggish henchmen as war criminals?

The more I watch America the more I am reminded of the Fall of the Roman Empire. The arrogance, conceit, racism and blindness to the needs, hopes, aspirations, expectations and rights of the rest of the world are all there. I fear for America. I fear that Americans are creating for themselves an isolated and fearful future.

345

English is the language of the English. The Americans do not have a language. There is no such thing as 'American'. If Americans spell English words a different way then they aren't 'different' they are simply 'wrong'.

346

Laws which are, it is claimed, there to protect women's rights are being introduced in the USA to ensure that although abortion may be legal it will soon be virtually impossible to obtain.

New laws relating to all aspects of the physical environment related to an abortion are being introduced and are known as TRAP laws (TRAP stands for Targeted Regulation of Abortion Providers). New laws are, for example, constantly being introduced to regulate the width of hallways, the height of ceilings and the angle of drinking fountains. Abortion clinics which fail to satisfy these laws are closed down, although other medical facilities (also used by women) do not seem to be expected to comply.

347

'America is at this moment developing advanced systems of 'weapons of mass destruction' and is prepared to use them where it sees fit. It has more of them

than the rest of the world put together. It has walked away from international
agreements on biological and chemical weapons, refusing to allow inspection
of its own factories. The hypocrisy behind its public declarations and its own
actions is almost a joke. America believes that the 3,000 deaths in New York
are the only deaths that count, the only deaths that matter. They are American
deaths. Other deaths are unreal, abstract, of no consequence.
The 3,000 deaths in Afghanistan are never referred to. The hundreds of
thousands of Iraqi children dead through American and British sanctions
which have deprived them of essential medicines are never referred to.'
HAROLD PINTER

348

Kenneth L. Lay, head of collapsed energy company Enron, was
major contributor to George W. Bush's presidential campaign. Mr
Lay was also an adviser to George W. Bush and to Dick Cheney
and it has been reported that he helped interview administration
appointees. Mr Lay is also said to have helped George W. Bush by
providing him with a list of preferred candidates for key posts on
the Federal Energy Regulatory Commission in the USA.

349

Virtually every national leader (except George W. Bush) disapproves
of recent Israeli action against Palestine. Throughout Europe twice
as many voters sympathise with the Palestinians as support the Israelis. In America the figures are more than reversed.

Readers who do not understand why America continues to support and defend Israel despite its horrendous war crimes against
the Palestinians should know that the rich Jewish lobby is enormously powerful and much feared in the USA.

The Jewish lobby in the USA controls much of the international media and shapes the Middle East debate in the USA. Americans have been convinced that Israel is a gutsy little democratic
country struggling to battle on against international terrorists – that
is what they are told by journalists and politicians.

The truth, (expressed recently in *The Economist* magazine) is that

'Israel is...a brutal occupying power with an essentially racist ideology'.

The curious thing is that Israel seems to be the only nation in the world not to have learnt anything from the holocaust. Maybe they have, for half a century, been living on the mixture of pity and goodwill which the holocaust generated. If they have then they should realise that the pity and goodwill are now exhausted.

When I had lunch with a British national newspaper editor recently he told me that he used to be a Zionist but that the activities of the Israelis had turned him into an anti-Zionist. 'The Jews may', he said, 'have taken some physical territory but they have succeeded in handing over the moral high ground to the Arabs.'

It is now clear that Israel has breached the laws of war. Israel's leaders should be brought before an international War Crimes Tribunal without delay.

It is clearly bizarre and unjust that Saddam Hussein should be attacked and Milosovic should be indicted for war crimes while Ariel Sharon isn't even criticised by the Americans.

The Israelis should be forced (through the UN) to relinquish illegal Jewish settlements and to vacate occupied Palestinian territory. The Security Council Resolution 242 which calls for Israel to withdraw is simply being ignored (though this does not seem to worry the Americans).

It becomes clearer day by day that the very founding of the State of Israel in 1948 was a terrible mistake. The Israelis have consistently abused international trust and must be held responsible for the continuing mayhem in the Middle East.

'Many American Jews are appalled by the recent military actions and some even believe that, given the intractabilities of the Middle East, Israel really should cease to exist,' said a writer in *The Economist* magazine.

350

Freedom may be disappearing fast in Europe but it has pretty well disappeared from view in the USA where more than 600 foreigners were detained in a relatively short period after 11th September 2001.

The USA Attorney General has refused to release the names of the people detained though it is known that an innocent doctor was rounded up because he had the same name as a hijacker and had stood behind another hijacker in a queue at a bank.

American authorities have now been given authority to monitor communications between federal prisoners and their lawyers and the American Justice Department plans to question 5,000 students from Muslim countries to find out whether they are terrorists. (Presumably asking questions such as: 'Are you a terrorist?' 'Are you planning to hijack any planes and fly them into buildings?')

Companies are obliged to report any purchase which involves over $10,000 in cash. Any foreigner suspected of terrorism can be detained and tried by a special military tribunal. There have been plans to detain foreigners indefinitely.

Most Americans apparently approve of and support these new laws. Many think that the proposals are too mild.

Why anyone visits the USA these days is quite beyond me. Business (if essential) can be conducted over the telephone or by fax. And there are plenty of much safer, more hospitable places for tourists.

351

'If anybody harbours a terrorist, they're a terrorist,' said the moronic and hypocritical George W. Bush. 'If they fund a terrorist they're a terrorist...if they develop weapons of mass destruction that will be used to terrorise nations, they will be held accountable.'

Er...George...er...George...are you really going to declare war on yourself?

352

The FBI recently announced that it had somehow managed to lose 449 guns and 184 laptop computers. At least one of the stolen guns has been used in a murder. And one of the stolen computers contains top secret intelligence information.

353

'They that can give up essential liberty to obtain a little temporary safety deserve neither liberty nor safety.'
BENJAMIN FRANKLIN

354

Back in March 1998, in an article headed 'Chips With Everything', I warned that American scientists were planning to insert microchips into people. The ghastly plan was, I said, for us all to have a single microchip stuck under the skin on our hands or arms – instead of having to carry around credit cards, bank cash cards, membership cards and so on.

The chips would, I wrote, also be used to carry medical information. And travellers wouldn't need to carry passports because their passport information would be carried in the chip under their skin. Quite a few people laughed. Many scoffed. Now the chip is here and the nightmare has become reality. The new under-the-skin microchip implant is electronically powered by body heat, has sensors to measure pulse and blood pressure and has a GPS satellite link so that the people controlling the chip will know exactly where everyone is all of the time. When you buy something you just flick your hand (and chip) across the scanner and the money will be taken from your account. (Of course if you're a robber you just chop off people's hands and you can go anywhere and be anyone.)

The idea is that we will all soon have one of these chips under our skin. They will, of course, be voluntary. But without one you won't be able to travel, get cash out of the bank or get hospital treatment. The manufacturers received a special technology award from the World Economic Forum in Davos, Switzerland.

355

Never before has a nation with so much natural wealth had so little humility, insight or respect for other cultures.

356

American special services began to help the Afghan Mujahidin in rebellion against the communist regime a full six months before the Soviet invasion of Afghanistan in 1979.

The CIA had, throughout this clandestine operation, knowingly increased the probability that Russia would invade Afghanistan. The Americans deliberately drew the Russians into a trap.

Between 1980 and 1989 the Afghan resistance received from the Americans nearly 15 billion dollars worth of military assistance. One of the rebel leaders who was supported by the Americans was a known drug trafficker. Washington covered up the drug trafficking (as they always do). The Americans even opened a recruitment centre for Islamist combatants in the middle of New York (the modern CIA makes Macchiavelli look positively decent and straightforward) and encouraged Muslim nations to send troops (either of the orthodox or guerrilla variety) into Afghanistan.

This fight had nothing to with America but their mistake in getting involved has changed the modern world.

One of the men encouraged to fight in Afghanistan (and trained by the CIA and given weapons paid for by the American taxpayers) was called Osama bin Laden.

After the Soviets withdrew groups of American sponsored warriors were set up and run by Pakistan, Saudi Arabia, Iran and India. The Afghans warned the Americans that having so many separate groups fighting in one country would backfire but the Americans assumed that all Muslims are, by virtue of their religion, going to fight together against godless communism. (Only the very ignorant and arrogant can be so absurdly naive.) The result was that America turned Afghanistan into a military free for all; a battlefield strewn with corpses and rubble.

The Americans did this all by themselves. It was their choice, their responsibility and their mistake. The Americans created the Taliban and the chaos that is modern Afghanistan. And they trained and 'created' Al Qaeda.

357

American Catholics have for decades actively opposed the use of birth control in poor, over-populated parts of the world. As a result millions of people die from starvation each year. (Despite their allegiance to the Pope, the Americans seemed happy to ignore the papal disapproval of the 2003 war on Iraq. The presence of oil can, it seems, overrule even the Pope.)

358

'Freedom of the press has (since about 1940) been only a half reality. After about 1960 it disappeared entirely. I speak as an ex 13-newspaper publisher. Today truth is found only in the alternative press, ie newsletters. But their power/circulation is minuscule against the millions whose only information source is mega-press, radio and TV. Still, the pamphleteers (early newsletters) beat the establishment in 1774-1776 and created great stir in 1770-1800 in France. So, perhaps there's hope. Meantime, believe nothing you read/hear in the mega-press/TV. By nothing I really mean nothing.'
CHEVALIER HARRY D SCHULTZ, AUTHOR AND PUBLISHER OF
HSL NEWSLETTER.

359

While Bush 'n' Blair denied that their war against Iraq had anything to do with oil, media magnate Rupert Murdoch was predicting that getting rid of Saddam Hussein would lead to a dramatic drop in the price of oil and an international postwar boom.

360

America told Europe and Japan to reflate their economies in order to protect the world from rocky times and to relieve the pressure on American businesses and farmers. It seems that the Americans aren't content to carpet bomb undeveloped countries; in addition, they are now trying their hand at economic dictatorship.

361

Before the attack of 11/9 America ignored terrorism abroad – unless it had a direct effect on American lives or property. In some cases Americans actively encouraged terrorism (as they did in Ireland).

After 11/9 American president George W. Bush decided that all terrorists were a threat to America. He announced that anyone not prepared to join America in attacking terrorists would be regarded as the enemy and he blurred the differences between such vastly disparate problems as those of Sri Lanka, Indonesia, Palestine and Northern Ireland. (In deference to the Irish vote in America the American government continued to support the terrorists in Ireland.)

The American line on terrorism gave politicians around the world an excuse to stamp down on local freedom fighters. The Russians, for example, received American blessing for suppressing revolutionaries in Chechnya. Even the meanest dictator could, with American approval, obtain American approval for the killing of his opponents simply by describing them as 'terrorists'.

362

The Americans (with British support) bombed Afghanistan on the basis that they were pretty certain that someone whom they thought was a terrorist and who might have been responsible for an attack on their country might be living there. (Next time you hear a celebrity moaning about press harassment just remember how effectively Osama bin Laden managed to hide his whereabouts.)

We should not be surprised at this display of belligerence. George W. Bush, who scurried off to safety when his country was attacked, is a long-term supporter of capital punishment and Americans have never been too concerned about the guilt or innocence of the people they execute (as long as they are poor and preferably not white).

The Americans haven't given the world any proof that Osama

bin Laden is guilty and they didn't seem to know if he was in Afghanistan but they bombed the country anyway in what must surely be one of the most despicable attacks in history. Innocent Afghans were left digging themselves out of the rubble of their homes in a sick mirror image of the way that American office workers were left scrabbling through the debris of the World Trade Centre.

As they always do when they organise bombing raids the Americans quickly ended up dropping bombs in the wrong places. On the very first night of the pseudo-war the Americans managed to kill four United Nations funded mine clearance workers who were asleep in their beds at the time.

In an attempt to sanitise these sustained acts of state terrorism the Americans (and, of course, Tony Blair) boasted that they were dropping food parcels from 30,000 feet onto the Afghanistan countryside.

What did the Americans consider to be essential food supplies for starving Afghans? Their first relief planes were dropping peanut butter and strawberry jam onto stretches of heavily mined desert. I hope the Americans remembered to include tin openers in the parcels. And napkins.

If it wasn't so cynical, so thoughtless and so cruel it would sound like something out of a Marx Brothers film. Only the Americans could have done this. Only Americans (and New Labour politicians in the UK) could attempt so ruthlessly to exploit public opinion with such a feeble attempt at propaganda.

When the Americans have finished in Afghanistan, and swagger back to Texas, there will probably be a civil war in Pakistan. The Americans paid $1 billion over the counter to the Pakistan Government for permission to use their country as a base for their bin Laden hunt. Plus, the leader of Pakistan (who had been widely criticised as a military dictator) suddenly found that all criticism of his regime had disappeared. He was, indeed, invited to take tea with both Bush and Blair.

The Americans have an extraordinary ability to screw up everything they touch and to leave chaos, bewilderment, frustration and bitterness behind them.

363

The Americans claim that Saddam has been supporting Al Qaeda for decades. But Al Qaeda has only been in existence for five years. Before that Osama bin Laden worked for the CIA.

364

Radiation levels in Iraq are dangerously high as a result of depleted uranium used by America in the Gulf War. Iraqi babies are born without brains, eyes or genitalia. Blood pours from their ears and mouths.

365

'Rarely is the question asked: is our children learning?'
GEORGE W. BUSH, PRESIDENT OF THE USA. YOU HAVE TO ADMIT THAT THE FOOL IS (THIS TIME) ALMOST CERTAINLY RIGHT. THIS IS PROBABLY NOT A QUESTION WHICH IS ASKED TOO OFTEN.

366

Using bulldozers supplied by the Americans the Israelis have destroyed more than 7,000 Palestinian homes since the beginning of the Israeli occupation of Arab land. As a result more than 30,000 Palestinians are homeless. In some cases houses were bulldozed while their Palestinian owners were still inside. This was done with American support and approval.

367

Since 1979 an American research group called Freedom House has measured press freedom around the world. The press in Norway now has the media with the greatest freedom. Burma, Iraq and North Korea have the least freedom, followed by Afghanistan, Cuba and Saudi Arabia. The UK comes a lowly 17th on the list and the USA is at no 15. Both are just above Burma and Iraq but still rather poorly placed when it comes to offering their citizens a free press.

368

Remember: the Russian army destroyed far more of the German army than the Americans did. It is important not to confuse American-made war movies with reality, though that is a mistake lots of uninformed Americans now seem to make.

369

'I understand small business growth. I was one.'
GEORGE W. BUSH, SHOWING SYMPATHY TO ENTREPRENEURS.

370

The Americans have demonised the Taliban (as they did with Colonel Quaddafi and Saddam Hussein and as they always do with opponents) but when a disguised British journalist was arrested the Taliban treated her with (in her own words) 'respect and courtesy' and returned her unharmed, after the bombing had started.

Would the British police have returned a citizen from Afghanistan who had entered the UK under similar circumstances? Without even a trial? Somehow, I doubt it. The British police don't even treat British citizens with 'respect and courtesy'. I am ashamed to say that I rather suspect that the British police would have beaten her up and then, when the bruises had faded, the Foreign Secretary would have handed her over to the Americans. Who would have promptly executed her.

371

Find a war and you'll find that both sides are fighting with weapons supplied (at a price to someone) by the American and British arms industries. When American or British troops are killed they are usually killed with British or American bullets fired from British or American guns.

Is more violence really the only answer? Where will all the violence end? When does state approved revenge become state sponsored terrorism? Is America justified in killing innocent people in Afghanistan because innocent people have died in America?

Instead of seeking revenge America should lead by example. Instead of retaliating in hatred they should ask for peace. Why does that thought seem so naive?

372

Terrorism is based on anger and intolerance. The Americans have not learned that it cannot be defeated by yet more intolerance.

373

American activities in Iraq and elsewhere have reinforced the conflict between Europe and the Muslim world and have helped establish strong fundamentalist Islamic politicians in power.

The American activities in the Middle East are invariably self serving: the aim is to satisfy the arms industry, the oil industry and the Zionists. The cost is stability and peace. Americans don't worry about the cost of war because war is usually profitable for the massive American arms industry.

374

It is nauseating and pitiful to see the Americans interfering time and time again in other countries. They invariably do this under the pretence that their activities are designed to protect the oppressed. Sadly, their activities are not guided by humanitarian principles but by self-interest; by their desire for control and by their economic aims. The Americans who direct these policies either don't care about the consequences or they are deliberately inciting trouble because in their own twisted and warped way they believe that America (and, in particular, corporate America) can benefit.

Everywhere they go the Americans create havoc and confusion. Their ill-timed, ill-directed military attacks (bombing civilians seems to be a speciality) inevitably result in more deaths than would otherwise have occurred. After a particularly bad night, during which many civilians (including, inevitably, a number of women and children) had been bombed to oblivion in Afghanistan by cheering American airmen, an American spokesman claimed that his country did not deliberately target civilians, as though there was some difference between civilians killed through incompetence and bad marksmanship and civilians killed through spite.

The American spokesman did not seem to understand that terrorism conducted by a large state is just as unforgivable as terrorism sponsored by a small state.

375

'The Iraqi regime is a threat to any American and to threats who are friends of America.'
GEORGE W. BUSH, PRESIDENT OF THE USA BUT STILL JUST A MIXED UP MORON AT HEART.

376

Inspired by the USA, British Foreign Secretary Jack Straw claims that Britain (and other countries such as America) should have the right to interfere in countries which are in danger of 'failing'. And the criteria for judging 'failing states'? Well, Straw says he will be looking for countries where there are areas of territory that a country is unable to control and where there are ethnic and religious tensions. Those, according to New Labour, suggest that a country needs to have its Government replaced. And Straw also suggests that 'corruption and failing public administration' might be signals of 'poor governance'.

Someone should remind Straw of the proverb about people in glass houses. The problems in Northern Ireland mean that the UK fits the first two criteria requiring international intervention. And the New Labour Government offers an excellent example of 'corruption and failing public administration'.

So, who is going to invade London and liberate the British people from the Blair tyranny? In the few years since he took over as leader, Blair has been at least partly responsible for three unnecessary wars. New Labour policy is increasingly looking like: 'If it's foreign – bomb it.' It is, I suppose, their clumsy version of colonialism.

377

American doctors kill more than 3,000 innocent Americans every day of every week of every month of every year. Those innocents often die in agony – after unnecessarily long and painful illnesses. When is the world going to hold three minutes silence for them?

378

More than two thirds of American senators do not possess passports and have not, therefore, ever been out of their own country.

379

The Americans and the British want to kill hundreds of thousands of innocent Iraqi citizens in order to protect them from their bloodthirsty leader.

It really doesn't make any sort of sense, does it?

380

Around 7,600 Americans die each year from internal bleeding caused by the long-term use of painkillers. That is more than twice the number of people who died in the infamous September 11th attack on America. There is, as yet, no evidence of the American government bombing the offices of pharmaceutical companies.

381

The use of the word 'niggardly' is no longer allowed in the USA. Astonishingly, the word is regarded as racially abusive. The dictionary definition of 'niggardly' is: stingy, meagre.

382

It is well worthwhile remembering that powerful Americans have a long history of manipulating local and world opinion. For example, it now seems that USA president Lyndon Johnson obtained Congressional approval for the war in Vietnam by using an incident which probably never occurred.

Johnson claimed that North Vietnam had attacked American warships in the Gulf of Tonkin and, as a result, Congress gave him approval to 'take all necessary steps, including the use of force' to help America's South Vietnamese allies.

Americans who were opposed to the war felt that they had no choice because America had been attacked. However, it seems that Johnson was 'misled' and the North Vietnamese hadn't fired at all.

383

Americans consume more oil and natural gas per capita than the citizens of any other country. They also consume more calories (which explains why most of them are disgustingly, grossly, unhealthily obese).

384

'Ariel Sharon of Israel is a Man of Peace.'
GEORGE W. BUSH, PRESIDENT OF THE USA, STRETCHING THE
IMAGINATION OF HIS LISTENERS.

385

Americans produce more waste than the citizens of any other country in the world. America produces twenty times as much hazardous waste as the number two on the list (Germany).

386

George W. Bush reneged on the USA's agreement with the E.U. to cut carbon dioxide emissions. The USA now produces more carbon dioxide emissions than Australia, Brazil, Canada, France, India, Indonesia, Germany, Italy, Mexico and the United Kingdom combined.

387

Warmongering American and British leaders are unlikely to be arrested or tried, but by all proper international standards and laws, it is difficult not to believe that they will eventually be regarded as war criminals.

388

During the last half a century America has consistently spent more money – and a greater percentage of its Gross National Product – on health care than any other developed country in the world. America is the home of high technology medicine. And Americans take more supplements and more 'wonder' remedies than citizens of any other nation in the world.

The effectiveness of this national obsession with good health can easily be measured for there are two simple and widely recognised ways to measure the quality of a nation's health care: the first is to measure life expectancy, the second is to measure the infant mortality rate.

The figures show that the American way simply doesn't work. Life expectancy in America has steadily fallen when compared to other countries and today America's infant mortality rate puts it 18th out of the 21 developed nations. Libya, Mauritius and the Seychelles all have a lower infant mortality rate than Detroit.

In addition, Americans suffer more from doctor-induced disease than any other country in the world.

389

Within months of entering the Oval Office, George W. Bush stepped up the drug war in South America. The Americans then helped the Colombians shoot down a plane full of American missionaries.

390

The United Nations has removed the United States of America from its Human Rights Commission because George W. Bush has defied UN human rights agreements.

391

When an American spy plane collided with a Chinese plane (over Chinese territory), knocking it out of the sky and killing the pilot, the American president (George W. Bush) refused to apologise but rudely demanded the return of the American plane which had had to land in China. What would the Americans have done if a Chinese spy plane had knocked an American plane out of the sky and then landed in Texas?

392

The South African Government was, for decades, allowed to develop weapons of mass destruction, murder opponents, engage in terrorism, attack neighbouring countries and violate many UN resolutions. The Americans did nothing. If anything they collaborated with and supported the South African regime. Both the USA and the UK have ignored human rights violations in Zimbabwe (which doesn't have any oil).

393

American oil companies pay the Islamic Government in Northern Sudan so that they can gain access to untapped oilfields there. And American Christian groups finance the non Islamic Southerners because they believe that in doing this they are helping to fight the war against Islam. The result: civil war, paid for pretty much entirely by Americans.

394

Under Bill Clinton's Presidency, America launched Cruise missiles on Khartoum, allegedly to destroy a pharmaceutical factory. (The Americans were presumably worried that the drugs made were cheaper than American versions.) No warning was given. The launch of the missiles happened (coincidentally, of course) just before a certain Monica Lewinsky was due to appear before a Grand Jury. Britain's New Labour politicians revere Bill Clinton; regarding him as a great man, a wonderful leader and an example to them all.

395

America spends more money on guns than any other country on earth. More Americas die from firearm injuries than citizens of any other country on earth. Americans still insist these two facts cannot possibly be linked.

In England and Wales there are 15 murders for every 1 million people. In the USA there are 55 murders for every 1 million people. American policemen are far more likely to be murdered than British policemen. And most of those murders involve guns. It is seven years since a police officer was shot dead in England. But around 50 policemen a year are murdered in the USA – nearly all of them killed with guns.

Americans claim that they have guns to protect their homes. But, when a gun is fired during a burglary, the burglar is hit only 2 per cent of the time. The other 98 per cent of the time the gun owner either shoots a relative or themselves or the burglar takes the gun and kills the gun owner.

396

Forty four million Americans are functionally illiterate. The average American spends 1,460 hours a year watching TV and just 99 hours reading books.

397

Seventy major American Universities run courses in English literature. Only 23 of those Universities require students to study Shakespeare. The reason why 47 universities ignore Shakespeare? Shakespeare isn't American.

398

The Americans have withdrawn from the Geneva Convention.

399

Tony Blair is known in diplomatic circles as George W. Bush's 'speak-your-weight machine'. He is known in Europe as Pinocchio. And the IRA's code name for him is 'Naive Idiot'.

400

A surprising number of George W. Bush's associates have links with the oil industry. National Security Adviser Condoleeza Rice, who formerly served on Chevron's board of directors, had a 130,000-ton oil tanker named after her.

401

If, as they claimed, the Americans knew that Iraq was hiding weapons they must have seen them and must have known where they were. Why did they not give this information to the weapons inspectors?

402

Largely thanks to the USA, over 11,000 species of plants and animals are now close to extinction.

403

'General Musharraf of Pakistan is a Democrat.'
GEORGE W. BUSH, PRESIDENT OF THE USA, PROVING THAT
HE HAS A MORE VIVID IMAGINATION THAN HAD BEEN
PREVIOUSLY ACKNOWLEDGED.

404

President Clinton excused Sports Utility Vehicles (SUVs) made by three big car makers from mileage requirements for ordinary cars. These cars use up an additional 280,000 barrels of fuel every single day. Because of that massive demand America now wants to drill in the Arctic National Preserve in Alaska.

405

Global air pollution causes 200,000 deaths a year. Most of that pollution comes from cars. Most of that car pollution occurs in the USA.

406

Two thirds of American graduates don't speak any foreign language. Not even a few words. Nothing.

407

America has introduced a first strike policy – giving itself the right to start wars whenever it feels like it.

408

The Americans have withdrawn from the agreement to create an International Criminal Court. And they have insisted that American servicemen are the only soldiers in the world who will be immune and cannot be prosecuted at the Court.

409

During the 1980s and 1990s the average household income in the USA stayed much the same when adjusted for inflation. But for the top 1 per cent of the population average incomes zoomed from $256,000 to $644,000 (adjusted for inflation).

The American poor are getting poorer. The middle classes stay the same. And the rich just get richer.

Rich Americans got richer during that period not because technology improved productivity but because poorer people had to work harder. American blue collar workers had to work 41 per cent longer hours than French workers and 28 per cent longer hours than German workers.

Americans who believed that improvement in share prices was a result of improved productivity and a better version of capitalism were fooling themselves. The improvement was as fake and as unsustainable as the improvement in Japan in the 1970s and 1980s which led to massive share price increases (and a subsequent decade long crash and deflation).

410

When it was suggested that a candidate from Thailand be considered for the Presidency of the World Trade Organisation, USA president Clinton threatened a permanent grid-lock unless America's chosen candidate was selected.

The WTO has been described by the UN as a nightmare for developing countries. The International Monetary Fund and the World Bank are similarly controlled by America and used to protect and develop American interests.

According to *The Economist* 'the Fund and the Bank...have become a more explicit tool of western, and particularly American, foreign policy.'

411

In 1983 the USA was alone at the UN in voting against a declaration that 'education, work, healthcare and proper nourishment and national development are human rights'.

In 1996 at a UN sponsored World Summit the USA rejected an affirmation that 'everyone has a right to safe and nutritious food'. The home of the 'harmburger' insisted that it does not recognise a 'right to food'.

412

According to the United Nations, the USA has consistently violated the World Convention against Torture. Both the Green Berets and the CIA are alleged to have routinely tortured prisoners and have trained other regimes in torture methods.

413

In 1986 the USA was condemned by the World Court for 'unlawful use of force' (aka 'international terrorism'). In the same year the USA vetoed a United Nations Security Council resolution calling all States (and this was aimed particularly at the USA) to adhere to international law. (When, in 2003, it was thought that Russia or France might veto a United Nations resolution giving America legal authority to bomb Iraq, the Americans said that if they did this it would mark the end of the United Nations. They also told the French that they would simply ignore their veto. 'We will not forgive and we will not forget,' president George W. Bush is said to have said to French president Chirac.) Britain's Prime Minister said he would ignore any number of vetoes (rather bringing into question the whole point of having a United Nations at all).

It is worth remembering that the USA has so far used its veto 73 times – three times under George W. Bush (mainly to protect Israel from criticism).

414

At the end of the Gulf War the Americans bombed a retreating Iraqi convoy which was showing the white flag. The Iraqis had surrendered. The Americans killed and buried alive 150,000 soldiers who had surrendered. If any other country had dared do that the military leaders involved would have been taken to a War Crimes Tribunal.

415

When trying to work up world enthusiasm for a war against Iraq, USA president George W. Bush got confused between Iraq and Iran; at one point describing the people of Iraq, led by Saddam Hussein, as Iranians. This led some commentators to wonder whether Bush really knew which country he was preparing to bomb to smithereens – and whether his generals would know which country to attack when they were given the order to start a war. Personally, I thought that maybe the UN should introduce a resolution forbidding national leaders from waging war against countries which they could not spell or find on a map. Such a resolution would probably limit America to waging war on Canada.

416

'George W. Bush is a clueless former alcoholic drink driver ... [who] now works for the corrupt corporate interests that secured his election to the White House in the first place'.
MICHAEL MOORE, AUTHOR OF *STUPID WHITE MEN*

417

The Americans regularly sell products (such as unsafe drugs and particularly toxic types of tobacco) to Third World countries.

418

Only two countries have refused to ratify the 1989 UN Convention on the Rights of the Child. Those two countries are America and Iraq.

419

In 2001 the USA was thrown off the 53 member Human Rights Commission because it was felt that its membership was inappropriate.

420

For decades the USA refused to pay its dues to the United Nations. When it finally agreed to pay it demanded a reduction in its assessments and then still refused to pay up. America is, as it frequently tells anyone who will listen, the richest country in the world. One eminent writer complained that the USA has 'exercised sustained, systematic, remorseless and quite clinical manipulation of power worldwide, while masquerading as a force for universal good'. It is, he added, 'arrogant, indifferent, contemptuous of International Law, both dismissive and manipulative of the United Nations: this is now the most dangerous power the world has ever known – the authentic 'rogue state', but a 'rogue state' of colossal military and economic might'.

421

In the 111 years between 1890 and 2001 the USA began 134 wars around the world. The wars were started to 'protect American interests overseas'.

422

The final bill for the 2003 war against Iraq could be £1,000,000,000,000. If one tenth of that sum was spent on providing hospitals, medicines, schools and food to nations where terrorism breeds there would be no Al Qaeda, no terrorists and no need for war.

If Bush 'n' Blair just wanted peace they could buy it for less than the dollar cost of war. That's the tragic truth.

But those leading the war against terrorism are concerned with power, oil, money and politics and not with eradicating the causes of terrorism. America prefers to spend its arms budget on killing people. It is, in the end, more profitable.

423

The USA has intervened militarily, and through covert action, in virtually every neighbouring country: Bolivia, Brazil, Colombia, Cuba, Dominica, Ecuador, El Salvador, Guatemala, Haiti, Honduras, Jamaica, Mexico, Panama, Peru, Surinam and Uruguay. These interventions, invariably done in the false name of 'freedom' have ended up securing markets for American companies.

424

In Chile in 1973 the Americans brought down the democratically elected government of Salvador Allende. President Allende was assassinated and thousands of his supporters tortured and murdered. The Americans then installed right wing dictator General Pinochet in his place. Yes, it was the Americans who put Pinochet in power.

425

Many American politicians have never travelled outside the USA and have little or no knowledge of international affairs. Most American citizens have never travelled outside the USA and obtain all of their knowledge of the rest of the world from a media which is controlled by powerful corporations which have little or no interest in informing their viewers and readers about foreign cultures. Instead the media pumps out a constant diet of superficial rubbish endorsing wealth, power and violence.

426

After the September 11th attack on the USA an American magazine printed this comment: 'We should invade their countries, kill their leaders and convert them to Christianity.'

427

In the UK the BBC broadcast a special half hour peak-time interview with American hawk Donald Rumsfield during the 2003 springtime discussions about the second Gulf War. They did not, as far as I am aware, broadcast a similar interview with the Archbishop of Canterbury or the Pope (both of whom had declared themselves against the war).

428

In George Orwell's classic book *1984*, Oceana (the country which is ruled by the original Big Brother) is constantly at war. The war means that there is a continual state of national emergency. And the national emergency justifies Big Brother's removal of all civil liberties. The war also directs anger (which might have been directed at the Government) towards the unseen enemy.

George W. Bush's 'war against terrorism' is classic Orwell. The enemy will never be defeated and so we are now permanently at war. There are no specific military objectives – so governments can introduce all sorts of new wars whenever they feel like it. Democracy, freedom and human rights have all been eradicated and replaced by identity cards. Greater powers have been given to the police, customs officers and security firms. In America the Home-land Security agency is above the law and does not have to account to anyone for how it spends its billions. It is immune from the Free-dom of Information Act. It has the power to detain people indefi-nitely just because it wants to. It can confiscate property without giving a reason. It can't be sued.

The new American Office of Cybserspace Security has unlim-ited rights to monitor telephone calls and e-mails. Free speech has disappeared − all in the name of the new perpetual war against terrorism.

We have all been assured that the only way we can preserve our freedom is to give it up. This is absurd.

Bush 'n' Blair claim that the vast majority of citizens in the USA and the UK support all that is happening. But then the vast majority of citizens in Oceana supported Big Brother too. The world really did change on September 11th. But it didn't change because of what the terrorists did. It changed because of the way the Ameri-can and British Governments responded.

429

America is turning itself into a huge prisoner of war camp − with no rights, no privacy, no freedom, but plenty of armed guards, se-curity checks and identity papers.

430

Shortly before he was elected president of the USA George W. Bush was photographed shooting doves. Most people think of the dove as the bird of peace.

Mr Bush's desire to kill doves seems alarmingly symbolic.

431

It should never be forgotten that a UNICEF study done in 1999 showed that USA led sanctions on Iraq had resulted in the deaths of 500,000 children under the age of five.

432

There have been no sanctions on Israel – which has consistently defied the United Nations and which has broken more international laws than Iraq.

Israel has flouted UN Resolution 242 (which urges Israel to withdraw from land it occupied in 1967) for over 30 years.

433

Americans consume over half of all the goods and services in the world.

434

America gives $3.5 billion a year to Israel – which spends most of that money on arms. That is $500 per Israeli in an area where that is pretty much the national average wage. Most of the arms Israel purchases are bought from American arms companies. The money not spent on arms is used to build new, illegal settlements on Palestinian land.

The USA steadfastly refuses to acknowledge (or use its financial power to try to halt) Israel's violence towards the Palestinians.

The money the USA gives to Israel makes up 40 per cent of America's entire foreign aid. Yet United Nations resolutions clearly define Israel's occupation of the West Bank, Gaza Strip and East Jerusalem as illegal.

435

American newspapers are so parochial that they regard news from out of State as 'foreign'.

436

Americans spend over $8 billion a year on cosmetics. That is $2 billion more than would provide basic health and nutrition for everyone in the world.

437

If the September 11th attack hadn't happened president Bush (and the Republican Party) would have been in deep trouble by 2003 – thanks to crashing stock markets and crumbling economies. The Twin Towers attack rescued Bush from political disaster. Americans like the idea of war and a president who talks aggressively wins votes. Bush is promoting war for the same reason that he promoted executions – both win elector approval.

438

Bush needed to start a war against Iraq for several reasons.

First, having failed to find Osama bin Laden, Bush needed to do something to show that he was a man of action. His aides decided that Hussein would do nicely in lieu of bin Laden.

Second (and most important): oil. Iraq has oil reserves of between 100 and 300 billion barrels – at least 10 per cent and possibly up to 30 per cent of the world's total. That's a lot of oil. (In contrast America's entire reserves are a mere 22 billion barrels.) Bush wants to own Iraq because then he will own Iraq's oil. A puppet Government will be installed and all will be wonderful. This development will also give the Americans the opportunity to distance themselves from Saudi Arabia – a country which has a few problems of its own and which also isn't entirely popular with human rights groups. Taking over Iraq will almost certainly be the start of a wider colonisation programme.

Third, Bush Junior wants to avenge his father's embarrassing adventures in Iraq a few years ago. The Americans like to describe the war to liberate Kuwait as another success. It was not, and in their hearts the Bushes know this.

439

The Americans must be the most belligerent people on earth. They fought to dispossess the Native Indians. They fought to get rid of the British. They fought each other in a brutal civil war. And they have continued to fight anyone and everyone.

440

The Americans don't seem to understand how highly other nations value their freedom and independence. When the British Empire was at its biggest and most powerful many nations (such as India and parts of Africa) were far better off financially than they are today. But would any of those nations exchange their situation today with the way things were a century ago? Not a bit of it.

441

The Americans don't understand it but huge parts of the world now regard globalisation as being the same as Americanisation. People everywhere believe (accurately) that the Americans want to colonise the world.

442

The Americans are absolutely, totally wrong in believing that people are envious of the American way of life. The reality is that people all around the world hate the Americans for trying to impose their hideous lifestyle on everyone else.

Millions believe that the Americans want to rule the rest of the world – and don't give a fig for non-American citizens. I think they're probably right.

443

During World War II the Nazis did not torture RAF airmen even though doing so would have provided them with much helpful information. They obeyed the Geneva Convention.

But the Americans have tortured prisoners of war captured in Afghanistan and have attempted to deflect criticism by claiming that the prisoners they had captured weren't really prisoners of war and weren't criminals either. (Just what they were the Americans haven't yet said.)

To many people this makes the Americans worse than the Nazis.

Just because America is the richest and most powerful nation on earth does not excuse their behaviour or give them the right to ride roughshod over traditional standards of human behaviour.

Who will be the first foreign leader to have the courage to suggest that Bush be dragged before a War Crimes Tribunal?

444

Bush and his generals do not seem to be familiar with *The Art of War* by Sun Tzu.

Sun Tzu knew more about waging war than anyone else in history. Generals unfamiliar with Sun Tzu's principles have invariably been beaten.

'...if our military and political leaders in recent times had studied this work of genius,' wrote James Clavell, 'Vietnam could not have happened as it happened; we would not have lost the war in Korea; the Bay of Pigs could not have occurred; the hostage fiasco in Iran would not have come to pass; the British Empire would not have been dismembered; and, in all probability, World Wars I and

II would have been avoided – certainly they would not have been waged as they were waged, and the millions of youths obliterated unnecessarily and stupidly by monsters calling themselves generals would have lived out their lives according to their own Karma.'

445

'Maybe we're seeing the beginning of the end of American supremacy. As they become poorer and more isolated maybe they will become less enthusiastic about interfering where their meddling isn't welcome.'
READER'S LETTER

446

America deliberately keeps down commodity prices, thereby damaging the earnings of developing countries. America has created a global economy which suits its needs. Rich Americans get cheap food while the producers of its raw materials starve.

447

'The Americans want to invade Iraq and control its oil because Saudi Arabia is crumbling and about to implode and the Americans need Iraq's oil. Bush wants another four year term (because his father didn't get one) and can't possibly get in if Americans have to pay more for their petrol.'
READER'S LETTER

448

The Africa Growth and Opportunity Act, signed by George W. Bush in 2001, is supposed to help African countries sell products to America in return for American firms getting concessions in Africa. In fact the Act defrauds African countries.

The American Government only allows African countries to

sell products which won't compete with American manufacturers. For example, coffee and sugar can't be sold into America. Small quantities of textiles can be sold into the USA but only if they are made with fabric produced in the USA.

In return for this absurdly insignificant concession America gets massive controls over African economies and has the right to sell all its products in African countries. Fair? Hardly. Fraud? Probably.

449

All around the world American companies dump American products at prices below the cost of production – thereby obtaining a monopoly position and helping to subsidise costs of products sold to developed countries.

450

America has put huge tariffs on key, specific agricultural items such as rice, sugar and groundnuts. These trade restrictions alone cost poor countries billions of pounds a year in lost foreign exchange carnings.

451

Every day of every month of every year poorer countries lose an astonishing £1.3 billion to the USA because of rigged trading rules. As a direct result of these rigged rules 30,000 children die every day from preventable diseases. Moreover, every day, an additional £40 million more goes from poor countries to America (and other rich countries) in debt and interest payments.

452

The USA has reneged on its promise to abide by the Kyoto Treaty

– though the original terms of the Treaty were hardly onerous as far as the USA was concerned. The Kyoto Protocol was negotiated by more than 160 nations in an (admittedly feeble) international attempt to halt global warming. A panel of eleven top American scientists, commissioned by president George W. Bush, advised the American government that global warming is a real problem and is getting worse. They also concluded that human activity is the main factor.

The damage done by global warming is easy to define. The North Pole has melted. Four of the six glaciers in Venezuela have melted. The famous snows of Kilimanjaro have pretty well disappeared.

The ozone layer in the earth's atmosphere protects us all from ultraviolet radiation which can cause cancer.

The hole in the ozone layer is caused by chlorinated fluorocarbons (CFCs). These are chemicals used in air conditioners and refrigerators and aerosol cans. The biggest cause of this damage are air conditioning units in American cars. The hole in the ozone layer is 10.5 million square miles. (To save you working it out that's nearly three times the size of Europe. We're not talking pinpricks here.)

The Americans (led by George W. Bush) rejected the Kyoto Protocol because it was considered 'inconvenient' for American businesses.

America now plans to increase (not reduce) emissions by 33 per cent by 2012. While the rest of world is trying to reduce pollution levels America is merrily increasing them.

George W. Bush explained that if America stuck to the Kyoto treaty, American electricity prices would have to rise – thereby harming the pockets of American consumers.

453

'We're going to have the best educated American people in the world.'
GEORGE W. BUSH, PRESIDENT OF THE USA, GETTING IT RIGHT FOR ONCE IN HIS LIFE.

454

The American/British alliance have taken advantage of their convenient war to spray the Afghanistan poppy fields with nasty chemicals which will destroy the crops and stop anything growing in the fields for five years. This is, of course, a similar earth scorching policy to the one which the Americans pursued with so little success in Vietnam. Agent orange and napalm were, I seem to remember, the most popular remedies of choice.

This policy is outrageously high handed and it won't work. It has been pursued in South America with a woeful lack of success. All it does is put up the prices of drugs on the street. If the Americans really want to do something about their drug problem they might be better occupied persuading the CIA to stop supporting drug smugglers. Countries where opium and coca are grown in great quantities are usually countries where these products are historically established, where they are a part of the local culture and where the natives have used the products for centuries without great harm coming to them.

It was, of course, Western chemists who turned relatively harmless opium into refined, more powerful heroin and relatively harmless coca leaves into cocaine.

The real irony here, of course, is that the Muslims don't approve of alcohol and yet Americans get very upset if they are prevented from drinking booze while living or working in Muslim countries.

The American decision to destroy poppy fields should be put in perspective: how would the Americans and the British feel if the Muslims decided to bomb all our distilleries, hop fields and vineyards to stop us producing alcoholic drinks? Aggrieved, perhaps? Might we not think that what we decided to grow had nothing to do with them? Might not our politicians suggest that if the Muslims have a problem with alcohol they should simply make sure that people in their own countries did not use it?

455

'When privacy is outlawed only outlaws will have privacy.'
CLAIRE WOLFE, AUTHOR

456

'If America didn't have such a 'Thank God I'm an American' mentality (I believe that patriotism, like religion, only results in bad feeling) they might not be mourning the events of September 11th. But do you really think it will change their decidedly uncivilised and undemocratic mentality? Fat chance.'
READER'S LETTER

457

I wonder how much enthusiastic supporters of the Bush 'n' Blair war on Afghanistan know about the Northern Alliance.

Here, according to American magazine *Newsweek* is the way that Alliance soldiers dealt with Taliban prisoners trapped in a basement: 'Alliance soldiers poured diesel fuel into the basement and lit it, assuming that any remaining Taliban would be killed by the fire and the fumes. But when workers on Thursday went into the basement of a pink, one storey building in the centre of the compound to take bodies out, they ran into more than 100 Taliban still alive in the cells. Two of the workers were wounded, and a third was abducted or shot. The alliance then spent Thursday afternoon dropping large artillery rockets into the basement.

'It was horrible,' said Hamid (one of the prisoners). 'The rockets were exploding in the hallway of the basement and we were all hiding in the cells. The stairway was just a pile of rubble and there were parts of bodies all over.'

Finally, on Friday, alliance troops (supported by the Americans) flooded the basement with water. 'We spent the night in the freezing cold water,' said Hamid. 'Those who could stand up survived, but there were a lot of wounded who couldn't stand, and they drowned.'

458

'Bush was responsible for a host of deaths when he was Governor of Texas. There were suggestions that some of those who were killed by the State *weren't guilty but were sacrificed because Bush knew that killing a few poor people would help him win the election. Now he's president he's at it again. This time he is risking all our lives. And to my astonishment and shame Britain's Tony Blair is helping him.'*

READER'S LETTER

459

For decades America's foreign policy has been concerned only with extending America's power and influence. The American people have done nothing to control their Government, largely because they have been constantly misinformed by their Government, a biased media and a movie industry which has a very strange and parochial view of 'good' and 'evil'.

460

Critics of America are attacked viciously. Those Britons who have dared criticise America's globalisation policy in recent years have been described (in the pro-American British press) as 'unpatriotic', 'nihilist', 'masochistic', 'defeatist', 'fascist', 'Stalinist', 'the handmaidens of Osama', 'worm eaten by Soviet propaganda' and 'people who hate people'.

461

One million American children under the age of five consume unsafe levels of organophosphate pesticides every day.

462

To the Americans, 'trade liberalisation' means that American multinationals can sell their goods into a country without any barriers. The American controlled World Trade Organisation and the

International Monetary Fund force developing countries to change their food and agriculture policies to suit American exporters. At the same time developing countries are barred from selling to America.

463

Because the Americans couldn't find, catch and string up Osama bin Laden when they thought he was in Afghanistan, they attacked the Taliban, demonising them as evil terrorists intent on taking over the world.

In fact although the Taliban were repressive they were only interested in controlling their own people. The Taliban actually condemned the attacks on America as contrary to Islamic law. The Taliban's worst crime (as portrayed by Tony Blair's wife) seems to have been their insistence that their women covered up their faces. (To those of us who have been over-exposed to Cherie Blair's inanely grinning features this does not seem like a particularly unacceptable notion.)

Incidentally, since the Americans have long supported Saudi Arabia, which seems to follow the same general principles as the Taliban, it seems pretty obvious that the reason given for American intervention in Afghanistan was a pretty clumsy lie.

464

America controls the International Monetary Fund and the World Trade Organisation.

For example, it was at America's insistence that the IMF forced Thailand and South Korea to allow more foreign ownership of their economies. As a result American companies ended up owning key sectors in those (and other) countries.

465

America claims to support freedom. But America will not allow countries which do not follow and support the American way to exist.

What sort of freedom is that?

Under American 'leadership' we are now losing the freedom we are supposed to be fighting for. Those of us who oppose America's imperialism are now fighting for nothing more than tomorrow.

466

A poll of world opinion leaders showed that two thirds of non-Americans felt that Washington's policies were fuelling resentment and anger against the USA. But the same poll showed that less than a fifth of Americans blamed their Government for any ill-feeling against their country. Unbelievably, the vast majority of Americans genuinely believe that they are disliked because they are rich and powerful. One American columnist claimed (apparently seriously) that America is hated because it is 'powerful, rich and good'. Another claimed that those who hate America are 'backward and corrupt...and envious'.

George W. Bush, America's idiot president, claimed that America was hated because of: 'our freedom of religion, our freedom of speech, our freedom to vote...'. He did not appear to be joking when he said this, though those who remember the farce of the Florida vote counting (or, rather, not counting) may find this vaguely amusing.

Resentment and jealousy are, it seems, the only factors to which the Americans can relate. One significant reason for this is the fact that there is little or no 'national' American media and the vast majority of American media outlets are exceedingly parochial in their outlook. Americans don't understand why they are the most hated people on earth because they don't understand how they are perceived, how their Government is perceived and how their Government's actions impact upon other countries.

467

The people who now describe themselves as 'Americans' actually stole their country from the Native Americans. They put the Indians in reservations (which got smaller and smaller). The Indians were civilised and spiritual but they had no guns and were an easy target. America was stolen by force.

At a meeting in New England in 1640 the following motions were put to the assembly.

1. The earth is the Lord's and the fullness thereof.
2. The Lord may give the earth or any part of it to his chosen people.
3. We are his chosen people.

Naturally the assembled bunch of smug, barbarians voted 'yes' to all these motions, and thereby sanctified (in their minds) the theft of a nation.

It was generally agreed that the Indians were savages with no rights and yet both the American constitution and the Declaration of Independence were based on texts devised and used by Native American Indians – texts which included fundamental ideas on liberty, freedom and even legislature.

The American Government signed 370 treaties with the Native Indians but violated provisions in every one of these treaties. The Americans now celebrate the theft of the country they call their own with a feast called Thanksgiving.

468

'If you know the enemy and know yourself, you need not fear the result of a hundred battles. If you know yourself but not the enemy, for every victory you will also suffer a defeat. If you know neither the enemy nor yourself, you will succumb in every battle.'
SUN TZU, THE ART OF WAR

469

'When plunder becomes a way of life for a group of men living together in society, they create for themselves in the course of time a legal system that authorises it and a moral code that glorifies it.'
FREDERIC BASTIAT, *THE LAW*

470

The Americans have launched a war on terrorism. They know well that it is impossible to win such a war. Terrorism will never end. You can't sign a peace treaty with terrorists. The American Government launched a war on terrorism partly for economic reasons and partly because it provided an excuse to fight a secret war on privacy and freedom. Other Governments (such as the British Government) simply climbed aboard the band-wagon.

471

The two Clintons were, between them, paid millions of dollars for their memoirs. When they were being investigated over corruption charges neither of them could remember anything.

472

'The issue today is the same as it has been throughout all history; whether man shall be allowed to govern himself or be ruled by a small elite.'
THOMAS JEFFERSON

473

The American Government hands out $200 billion a year in corporate subsidies – including $25 million a year to the tobacco industry.

474

It used to be the case that our society preferred to see 100 guilty men go free rather than to see one innocent man be convicted wrongly. Now we are all considered guilty. Government employees all regard us as guilty – even when we are proved innocent. If we leave our homes we are photographed, recorded and searched. Whatever happened to privacy and freedom?

475

America has become a vast penal colony with more of its citizens in prison than any other country in the world. When Bill Clinton was first elected president of the USA there were about a million people in American prisons. By the time Clinton and his wife had skipped with the furniture from the White House there were two million people in American prisons.

Most American prisoners are black and impoverished and in prison for using drugs.

The war on drugs still continues – and is still a complete failure. In the USA the drugs war is responsible for a quarter of the two million Americans currently held in prison. Rich drug addicts tend to get put on recovery programmes. Poor drug addicts go to prison. Rich, white collar criminals tend to get small fines and modest sentences. Poor, blue collar criminals get long sentences.

476

'A low voter turnout is an indication of fewer people going to the polls.'
GEORGE W. BUSH, PRESIDENT OF THE USA,
SHOWING YET AGAIN WHY HE IS SO WIDELY
REGARDED AS A SIMPLETON.

477

The USA regularly targets civilian infrastructures when it wages war on another country. It deliberately bombs power plants, water treatment facilities, hospitals, schools, embassies, Red Cross buildings, transportation facilities, sewage facilities and so on.

In the Vietnam War the Americans carpet bombed three countries (Vietnam, Laos and Cambodia) and killed at least three million innocent civilians.

In North Korea the Americans carpet bombed the entire country. The media hid all this from the public.

478

'The press, once a freedom defender, now preserves our slavery.'
CHEVALIER HARRY D.SCHULTZ,

479

In American shopping malls, teenage girls give free cigarettes to youngsters to persuade them to start smoking.

480

Countries (such as Argentina) which tie their currencies to the dollar can get into big trouble. Argentina went bankrupt because it accepted dollars for everything it sold and then, when there were signs of a crisis developing, the rich Argentinians cashed in their local currency for dollars and sent the dollars to their American banks.

America sets interest rates according to its own domestic needs but has a currency which has an international aspect. Mexico's financial system collapsed because the USA raised interest rates very high.

Poor countries are encouraged to borrow to invest in development. But they cannot compete with international companies and their debt burden grows and grows. In the end they owe America more than they can earn.

If the dollar collapses it will not be America which will suffer (the Americans can simply print more dollars) it will be the countries which have sold their goods and services for dollars and which hold their reserves in dollars.

481

Americans now regard English as their language. They regard their spelling and grammar as correct − even though the 'language' they speak is often a grossly bastardised version of the correct version.

482

The American movie industry sells its products in other countries around the world at a below cost price. It can afford to do this because production costs are covered by American sales. (In addition, American films and television programmes are now regularly sponsored. Multinationals pay huge sums to have their products 'placed' in programmes.) The foreign sales are icing on the cake. The result of this policy is that other countries no longer have movie industries because home grown movie companies simply cannot compete on price.

America also dumps its TV programmes on other countries − thereby destroying local production companies. Programmes with high production values are sold for next to nothing. The Americans still make a profit but local writers, directors, actors and studios cannot compete and so go bust.

In contrast, American cinema houses and TV companies will, by and large, show only American products. If a film is a success in another country the Americans will remake a version of their own − replacing the original talent with their own.

All this helps to ensure that only American stars and products get global exposure.

The French have for decades had rules to protect their film, music and TV production industries. French cinemas and French TV stations are legally obliged to show a certain number of French-made films. National film-makers outside the USA need support to protect them. Other Governments should follow the French example. Otherwise it won't be long before the only home-grown productions are quiz shows, gardening programmes and cookery programmes.

483

I don't trust Saddam Hussein. But I don't trust George W. Bush either. And George W. Bush has more guns, bigger bombs and more supplies of nerve gas than Saddam Hussein.

484

It's curious how often politicians (such as George W. Bush and Tony Blair) claim that they want to wage war to preserve peace.

485

The USA demonises Iraq for having supplies of biological and chemical weapons. But the USA has the world's largest stockpiles of smallpox, anthrax and other biological weapons. The USA has 30,000 tons of chemical weapons. And the USA has consistently refused to support any UN initiative that would ban the development of biological and chemical weapons. The USA wholeheartedly supports the development of these weapons – as long as no other country is allowed to have them.

486

The USA spends nearly $400 billion a year on defence – half of all the military spending in the world. The USA maintains its position in the world solely through military might. This is how bullies traditionally operate.

487

In the last fifty years the USA has perverted elections and interfered with the democratic process in 23 countries.

488

America regularly imposes trade sanctions on other countries – to protect American companies. During the last 80 years America has imposed sanctions on 120 occasions – some of them long lasting. Recently, for example, the USA had active sanctions running against 75 countries.

489

With very few exceptions (such as British Royalty) Americans do not accept or acknowledge celebrities from other cultures – however successful those individuals may be. (The best selling recording artist in the world is probably not Michael Jackson or Elvis Presley or, indeed, any American, but Lata Mangashtar, an Indian female singer.) The Americans do not willingly acknowledge the existence of anyone not born in the USA.

490

When told that it will be boiling hot in the desert in the month of March (and therefore rather uncomfortable for fighting and sitting in tanks) an American general replied: 'Well, it will be the same for them, won't it?'

It did not seem to occur to him that Arabs might be better able to cope with the heat than soft, plump American servicemen.

491

'Last month a worldwide survey was conducted by the UN. The only question asked was 'Would you please give your honest opinion about solutions to the food shortage in the rest of the world?' The survey was a failure. In Africa they didn't know what 'food' meant. In Eastern Europe they didn't know what 'honest' meant. In Western Europe they didn't know what 'shortage' meant. In China they didn't know what 'opinion' meant. In the Middle East they didn't know what 'solution' meant. In South America they didn't know what 'please' meant. And in the USA they didn't know what 'the rest of the world' meant.'
READER'S LETTER

492

Even Americans admit that Europeans are the greatest biotech trailblazers. Whatever you think of genetic engineering, test tube babies and medical research the most important advances were made in Europe. In 1998 the EU passed a directive allowing scientists to patent human genes. Some governments (including those in France and Germany) refused to accept the law. Others (Italy and the Netherlands) are trying to get the law overturned. Even European scientists regarded the law as unacceptable and refused to join the 'land grab'. The Americans do not have any such qualms. American genetic engineers and American companies are now busy patenting human genes – and tests and treatments associated with those genes. Appalled and disgusted and defiant European geneticists are refusing to acknowledge the patents and pay the American companies which are looking to charge huge fees for tests and treatments built around the patents they have grabbed. The end result of the American 'land grab' will be that millions of patients will be unable to afford tests or treatment. When tests do prove worthwhile countless thousands will die because of corporate America. I have no doubt whatsoever that the eventual death toll will dwarf the deaths which were the result of terrorist action on September 11th.

Are lives lost due to the greed of corporate America of any less value than the lives lost due to acts of terrorism?

493

I no longer travel by plane. I'm not particularly worried by the terrorists. But I am worried by the loony security measures which now make flying an absurdly time consuming and unpleasant procedure.

One of the daft things about the so-called security checks is that the plastic explosive Semtex can be taken through airport security scans as easily as a pair of tights. Semtex has an indefinite shelf life, is far stronger than TNT and is apparently readily available on the black market. The world stockpile of Semtex is now put at 40,000 tons. Syria, Libya, North Korea, Iraq and Iran are said to have bought around 2,000 tons from the Communist Government in Czechoslovakia. Pan Am flight 103 was brought down over Lockerbie by just 12 ounces of the stuff.

Airlines are still confiscating nailfiles and nail scissors from would-be passengers. (I guess they are terrified that someone might rush into the cabin and cut the pilot's fingernails). But they still sell bottles of booze to passengers. They obviously don't realise that if you break a bottle it makes an excellent weapon. And they don't seem worried about passengers stuffing a piece of cloth down the neck and creating a Molotov cocktail. (They presumably don't worry about this because they know it is contrary to airline rules to open a bottle you've bought on the plane.)

The stupidity of security procedures is shown by the fact that not long ago two Irishmen got onto one plane carrying a leaky five gallon drum of petrol. Security presumably let them take it on board because it was clear that they couldn't possibly cut or file anyone's nails with it.

On another flight security officials allowed a passenger to board an aeroplane with a live hand grenade. Once again security officers were presumably satisfied that the grenade was of no danger because it offered no nail trimming facilities.

494

For those worried about biological warfare the greatest threat is probably smallpox. When the disease was officially conquered a couple of decades ago scientists kept stocks of the virus to 'play with'. The Soviet Union decided to turn smallpox into a weapon and had 60,000 scientists in 50 laboratories working on it. When the Cold War ended, the laboratories were closed and the scientists scattered. Some went to the USA, others to Iraq, Syria, Libya and North Korea. Did any of these scientists take samples of the smallpox virus with them? Probably. The wise thing would have been to destroy every last smallpox virus. This problem was predictable. I used the threat of a new smallpox epidemic as a subplot in a novel in the early 1980s.

495

'When the events of September 11th began to unfold I watched with disbelief,' wrote one reader. 'I desperately wanted to reach to the victims and their families and hug them close. I am still in shock, as I suspect that most of the world is. Then I read one of your articles about America and it did not make me angry at all. I am going to explain why.

It was one Friday night, in London at 10 pm, when our house was rocked on its foundations, and the windows were almost blown out. We were very lucky. The bomb had been primed wrongly. The IRA had intended it to go off at 10 am on a Saturday morning, when the local market would have been packed with families and teenagers.

The second bomb went off a few months later on the local train pulling into the station. The first few carriages of the train were shattered and people were killed. I heard NORAID mentioned for the first time and said, 'Don't be so ridiculous. America is our friend. They wouldn't support terrorism.' Again it was only in the next street from where we lived. Some local Americans wrote to our paper and claimed it was our fault for being in Ireland.

The third bomb, again locally, was planted on the step of our police station.

In spite of NORAID I do not hate the Americans. I hope that now the Americans will begin to understand that terrorism is terrorism, whatever the country.'

496

The mayor of New York has announced that the city of New York will give up recycling glass and plastic. Recycling is, apparently, too expensive for New York. (New Yorkers are presumably happy to let the rest of the world pay the environmental price.) I didn't know New Yorkers were so hard up. Maybe we should send them food parcels.

497

While Bill Clinton was president, America executed a man with the mental age of seven.

When the man (Ricky Ray Rector) was taken to the lethal injection chamber a guard asked him why he hadn't finished his last meal. 'I'll finish it when I get back to my cell,' replied Rector.

Clinton gave orders to execute this man because he (Clinton) was facing an election and needed to be seen to be strong on law and order.

As George W. Bush knows, a few executions do tend to bring the votes in.

498

I'm not accustomed to feeling sympathy for large corporations but there's always a first time. In America lawyers are now pursuing numerous companies (and their insurers) over asbestosis related claims. Most of the alleged 'victims' do not have asbestosis but are suing because they *might* have been exposed to asbestos in the past. If the lawyers win companies are likely to have to pay out up to $275 billion over the next 20 years. These lawsuits will probably mean that many companies will go bankrupt. The bottom line is that thousands of genuine patients won't get a penny.

(American workers who claim they didn't know that asbestos was dangerous should know that the first asbestosis compensation case took place in England in 1906. The asbestosis sufferer won.)

499

Fat Americans are now suing burger restaurants. They claim that they should have been warned that eating burgers and chips would make them fat.

500

When Tony Blair cared enough about the electorate to at least make soothing sound bites one of his pet slogans was: 'Tough on crime and tough on the causes of crime'.

Blair should dig out that slogan and take a long, hard look at it. There is little point in simply battering terrorism without dealing with the inequalities and injustices which lead to it.

But politicians, despite the rhetoric, aren't much interested in inequalities or injustices. Where's the money to be made?

If politicians were interested in injustices, and if they cared for their citizens, they would be tackling the big issues.

The wars against the chemical industry, the food industry, the tobacco industry and the drug industry controlled medical establishment are far bigger and far more crucial wars than the one against terrorism.

501

Some Americans seriously seem to believe that killing Osama bin Laden or Saddam Hussein will eradicate the problem of international terrorism. That is self-deluding nonsense. Millions of angry, frustrated people are ready to die for their beliefs. This is a war America (and Britain) cannot win through force and should not be fighting with guns.

The only real answer to the threat of terrorism is for our governments to pay attention to the causes: the prejudices, the conceit, the deceit and the widespread hunger and poverty caused by the selfish globalisation policies practised by the Americans.

Christians and Muslims have to share this planet. At the mo-

ment it is the only one we've got. We can only do that in peace
through learning mutual respect.

502

*'An American friend recently complained that I had spelt World Trade
Centre wrongly. He claimed that it should be spelt World Trade Center.
I pointed out that English is our language and that the inability of
Americans to spell properly does not mean that we must pander to
them. Actually, the name of the buildings which were destroyed was
a typical American act of hubris. The building may possibly
have been the American Trade Centre. It was never the
World Trade Centre.'*
READER'S LETTER

503

'Never trust any government anywhere; never, never, never.'
J.G. MURRAY

504

*'There can't be an American way to spell English words (such as 'colour')
any more than there can be an English way to spell French words. It is
absurd that Americans should attempt to study or teach English.
They can't even spell properly.'*
READER'S LETTER

505

The rumours that the American president and/or his staff knew
about the September 11th attack before it happened eventually
reached the USA Congress. 'What did this administration know
and when did it know it, about the events of September 11th? What

do they have to hide?' asked USA Congressman Cynthia McKinney.

We still have no answers.

Did George W. Bush know about the September 11th attack? Did his Government plan the attack? Or did they just let it happen? Did Tony Blair know?

All we know for sure is that the September 11th attack on America has given both Bush 'n' Blair an opportunity to introduce dozens of freedom crunching laws.

506

Approximately 12 per cent of all research work done in America is fraudulent.

507

One third of all medical spending in the USA ($600 billion a year) is for unnecessary, out-of-date and probably dangerous treatments. Few areas of 'purchasing' are as ineffective and as incompetent as those within the field of medicine. The problem is compounded by the fact that doctors and hospitals are both judged by, and paid for, the volume of business they do rather than the quality or results of their care.

508

Americans still insist on referring to Paris, France and London, England as though the American versions of these cities are of any real consequence. In future when I refer to New York or Washington I intend to write New York, USA and Washington, USA.'

READER'S LETTER

509

'We have a firm commitment to NATO, we are a part of NATO. We have a firm commitment to Europe. We are a part of Europe.'
GEORGE W. BUSH, PRESIDENT OF THE USA, PROVING THAT A GRASP OF GEOGRAPHY ISN'T ESSENTIAL FOR AN AMERICAN PRESIDENT.

510

A former US Army officer, performing weapons checks in Iraq for the United Nations, allegedly refused to do tests for biological weapons. He said he never expected to find any biological weapons and didn't want to give the Iraqis the benefit of a negative reading.

511

America's leaders have told the American public that if Saddam Hussein has weapons of mass destruction he will give them to Osama bin Laden to use on the American people.

This is nonsense. America's leaders are dishonest to make this claim. And Americans are stupid to believe it.

Saddam Hussein is a secular leader who has for years fought to crush Islamic fundamentalists in Iraq. He is no friend of Osama bin Laden. If he suddenly had a fit and gave weapons to bin Laden the chances are that bin Laden would use the weapons on him.

What the American people do not seem to realise is that by attacking Iraq America will unite the Muslims behind Osama bin Laden and trigger a long-term war for which they simply do not have the stomach.

If the American people really want peace, and want to be left alone by terrorists, they are going about things in precisely the wrong way. Their leaders are, for economic reasons of their own, leading them into the sort of perpetual war that terrifies them.

512

'The USA has about 50 per cent of the world's wealth but only 6.3 per cent of its population. In this situation we cannot fail to be the object of envy and resentment. Our real task in the coming period is to devise a pattern of relationships which will permit us to maintain this position of disparity without positive detriment to our national security. To do this we will have to dispense with all sentimentality and daydreaming, and our attention will have to be concentrated everywhere on our immediate national objectives. We need not deceive ourselves that we can afford the luxury of altruism and world benefaction. We should cease to talk about such vague and unreal objections as human rights, the raising of living standards and democratisations. The day is not far off when we are going to have to deal in straight power concepts. The less we are then hampered by idealistic slogans, the better.'
GEORGE KENNAN, USA STATE DEPARTMENT OFFICIAL, IN 1948

513

The 1991 Gulf War ended on February 28th. Iraq and the United States of America agreed to a ceasefire. Two days after the ceasefire, on March 2nd, thousands of Iraqi soldiers were deliberately killed (murdered is a perhaps more appropriate word) by American soldiers. No Americans were ever taken before a War Crimes Tribunal, although this was, without a doubt, one of the most horrendous war crimes ever recorded and almost certainly worse than anything the Americans did in Vietnam. If Iraqi soldiers had cold-bloodedly murdered thousands of Americans after an agreed ceasefire the responsible Iraqi military and political leaders would undoubtedly have been executed by enraged Americans.

At the end of the war the Americans (for reasons of their own) ensured that Saddam Hussein remained in power. Not surprisingly (and, perhaps, not entirely inaccurately) Saddam Hussein then declared that he had beaten the USA.

514

The Americans seem to want to own everything – including your body – and at the rate they are going they soon will.

American patent law is now so pliable (and American influence over the rest of the world so great) that there seems little doubt that a few major drug companies will, between them, soon own our bodies.

One company alone (Human Genome Sciences) is said to have patents on most of the 70,000 human genes.

An American company has been given a patent on all human blood cells obtained from the umbilical cord of new born babies. In the past, these cells were used without charge to treat other patients. In the future, licence fees will have to be paid to the company which has the patent on these human cells. (How long before someone patents the gene for red hair and then claims a royalty from the parents of every red-haired child?)

Many companies are patenting raw genetic data without having any idea of the value of what they are patenting. It's a gold rush but no one yet knows which are the gold nuggets and which are the worthless bits of stone.

One big American company has allegedly already refused to share its findings with publicly funded researchers.

It is now commonplace for American doctors to claim to own potentially life-saving medical procedures.

Even our own human genetic make-up is being snapped up by greedy doctors and scientists turned entrepreneurs. One third of the human genome which has so far been mapped is privately owned. A staggering eight thousand USA patents have been issued on human genes and methods and techniques related to their existence. Like it or not we are likely to wake up one day soon and find out that our bodies are owned by Americans. Fall over and graze your arm and you'll have an American lawyer on your doorstep claiming $5 million because you've damaged his property.

Already, in the USA, hospitals are fighting researchers about who owns new treatments, and genetic engineering firms are spending fortunes on lawyers as they claim patents over bits and pieces of the human body.

American courts have even stopped doctors prescribing life-saving treatments when rival companies have claimed to own part of the underlying technology. For example, cancer patients in the USA have been refused treatment with a drug made by one company because a second company claims its rights are being infringed – even though it does not have an alternative drug to offer.

Two things – apart from greed and an absence of any sense of public responsibility among American doctors, scientists and businessmen – are helping to make this greed-fest into a serious problem.

First, the rules about obtaining patents have changed in the USA. In the old days you could get a patent if you came up with a new type of wheel. These days you can even get a patent (and therefore a monopoly) on the idea of having a wheel. (You probably think I'm exaggerating. I'm not. USA patent No 5,707,114 is entitled 'Vehicle Wheel' and is for exclusive rights to the wheel, including: 'an annular rim, a central hub and a plurality of spoke portions running between the rim and hub.')

When one American company applied for patent protection for its genetically modified cotton plant it was given a patent for all genetically engineered cotton – however it was made. If most varieties of cotton in the future are genetically engineered then that company will have, effectively, patented cotton.

An American eye surgeon patented a particular type of cataract operation – and told other surgeons that they would have to pay a royalty every time they wanted to perform the procedure. One doctor owns the rights to a basic suturing technique. Another has the rights to the technique of making a slit in a skin graft in order to expand it. One doctor has patented the practice of applying the anaesthetic lidocaine to the skin to treat nerve pain associated with shingles. Another American doctor owns the right to the idea of treating a nosebleed with a catheter wrapped in gauze. A doctor has a patent on a technique to treat haemorrhoids. (If you are shocked and horrified by all this you may need to take a break before you continue reading. It gets worse.)

A radiologist in the USA has a patent covering the technique for determining the sex of a foetus aged twelve to fourteen weeks with ultrasound. The patent relies upon the radiologists ability to distinguish male genitalia from female genitalia. Although one radiologist compared this to having a patent to tell your right hand from your left, and another likened it to having a patent on the ability to distinguish the gender of patients when they remove their clothes, the patent is legally enforceable.

Human cells have been patented and genetic engineers claim that it won't be long before genetically engineered humans will be made. When that happens it seems reasonable to assume that the companies responsible for the technology will legally own those human beings. The USA government has ruled that anything under the sun that is made by man can be patented. So, a genetically engineered human can certainly be patented.

A researcher who has a patent based on an observation that elevated levels of human chorionic gonadotropin in pregnant women can signal the presence of a foetus with Down's syndrome sues doctors and laboratories that don't pay him a royalty on his observation.

One of the first and commercially most successful patents was for a breed of mouse that was genetically designed to get cancer. (As an aside, what brand of human being deliberately creates an animal that is designed to get cancer?)

Thanks to the American laws an application for a patent on the treatment for a rare genetic disorder means that a Swiss drug company now owns a patent on all ex-vivo human gene therapy. Today, scientists can get such broad patent rights that no one can repeat their experiments to check the results. One large American company has a patent giving it exclusive rights to any and all genetically altered soybeans, 'created by theirs or any other method that might be developed'.

American companies have now successfully claimed exclusive rights to a colour, to sounds and to smells. Lawyers believe that athletes can patent moves or techniques they use in competition. So, for example, a high jumper who devises a new technique could take out a patent. Or a golfer could patent the idea of chipping over bunkers instead of into them.

The system in America is now so crazy that a patent system critic who wanted to show the stupidity of the system managed to get a patent on Kirchhoff's Law – an 1845 scientific theory which states that the electric current flowing into a junction equals the current flowing out.

An American mathematician has a patent on two numbers –

and he has the legal right to sue anyone who uses his numbers without his permission. A publisher in one American state has exclusive rights to distribute and sell the electronic version of the state's laws.

Much of the information now being patented is paid for by American taxpayers (who contribute $60 billion a year towards basic research at universities and national laboratories). American taxpayers are paying for many of these research discoveries but private individuals and multinational corporations are taking out the patents and will ultimately be the ones to benefit. (Although, in the short-term, as you can imagine the people who benefit most from all this are the already far-too-wealthy American lawyers.)

There has been a collision between capitalism and democracy, and democracy has definitely come off second best.

Knowledge is power but ordinary people are now being denied access to knowledge.

'People who mean to be their own governors must arm themselves with the power which knowledge gives,' said James Madison, probably not realising when the time would come when ordinary people would no longer be allowed to take the knowledge route to self-governance.

The second big problem is the fact that American companies are frequently claiming world rights. And because the American government is owned and controlled by large companies those rights are usually upheld through trade threats.

The usual threat runs along the lines of: 'If you don't agree that this American company owns rights in your country then we won't allow any more imports from your country.' The Americans, never famous for their taste, sensitivity and culture, are as subtle as a brick when it comes to money.

America needs the rest of the world (both for its raw materials and as a market place for its products) and yet Americans abuse, rape and pillage apparently without shame.

More than 80 per cent of patents held in third world countries are owned by foreigners – mostly by global corporations based in the USA.

Drug companies are, for example, now claiming exclusive ownership of medicines and techniques which have been used in the Far East for centuries.

When a citizen of Ecuador discovered that an American had obtained ownership right to a plant species which is a key ingredient of a sacred hallucinogenic drink which has for centuries been used throughout the Amazon in religious ceremonies he complained that it was like an Amazonian travelling to America and claiming exclusive rights to communion wafers.

Drug companies are busy patenting plants all over the world – comforted by the knowledge that whereas 25 per cent of all prescription medicines are currently derived from plants only 10 per cent of the world's plants have been studied for medicinal qualities.

Looking for a quick way to get very rich? Take out patents on a bunch of plants you dig up in some out of the way stretch of jungle – and then sit back and wait for a drug company to find a use for one of 'your' plants. It is, of course, hard luck on the 80 per cent of the world's population who rely on wild plants for their medicinal needs.

The going rate paid by drug companies when buying up 'rights' is roughly $100 a species. Since a plant which proves to be useful can easily be worth $1 billion a year you might think that the drug companies are ripping off small, undeveloped countries.

There is, of course, no small irony in the fact that when America was a young country its citizens flagrantly ignored other countries' laws dealing with patents and copyright: many inventors and authors lost out as their creative work was hi-jacked by Americans.

The arrogance of the Americans is exhibited by the fact that when researchers claimed a patent on a drug traditionally used in Asia to make wounds heal faster their application was approved. The Americans decided that they would give patents to those claiming them unless it could be established that the substance in question had already been known or used in America. How's that for a sickening and obscene example of colonialism and parochialism?

To claim ownership of natural phenomena, the nature of health and ill health and the structure of the human (or any other living body) is grotesque and obscene; it is a restriction of human freedom and an example of a combination of the worst kind of selfishness and the most rapacious type of greed.

Patents on laws of nature are, in my view, an abuse of the system of copyright and ownership.

What is there to stop someone from patenting the law of gravity and then claiming royalties from those of us who benefit from it?

It seems that a sense of social responsibility no longer exists.

It is not only the patent owners who are to blame for what is going on. The society in which they operate, and which allows them to patent these things, must also take much of the blame.

Also worrying is the fact that this new trend means that research and development must inevitably be constrained. Software specialists claim that patents which have been allowed on lines of code make it nigh on impossible to create new programs.

'It is,' said one expert, 'like a carpenter having to pay a royalty every time he picks up a hammer or a saw.'

One large company recently won a patent for a method of searching for a word in a document that some argue has been in place for nearly three decades.

Another company has a patent on the software to move investment funds among different types of account.

Yet another has a patent on the ability to determine the amount of time a slide or transparency is viewed in a presentation. And on it goes.

One company has a patent on financial transactions on the internet – and many other major companies have agreed to license the patent.

Another company has a patent on the concept of electronic shopping carts, used by customers to pick up items as they browse through a web site. Yet another company has a patent covering secure, real time payment using credit and debit cards over the internet.

Many of these patents are widely infringed. I suspect that as internet companies start making money so the legal letters will start arriving.

(Americans have already patented vast parts of the English language so the lawyers could end up paying royalties too.)

'Ultimately,' writes Seth Shulman in his book *Owning the Future*, 'the principles we establish to assure public access to the conceptual commons matter more than the speed of technological development or the enormous sums of money that can be leveraged from the private control of knowledge assets. They matter because, whether we are studying the human genome, surfing the Internet, or displaying a digital image of the Mona Lisa, we in a democratic society have the right to shape our own future. And, whether we face a threat to our public lands, to the availability of clean water, or to access to information, we have the right and the responsibility to protect the precious assets in the public domain. If we fail, we will relinquish, erode, and eventually lose our public voice. And in a democratic society, even a wealthy one like ours, this may be our most precious asset of all.'

It is perhaps significant that virtually the only people supporting the new interpretation of patent laws in the USA are lawyers. 'Let them all sue each other,' said one lawyer, adding that it sounded like Nirvana to a guy like him.

This whole, sad and patently offensive story is an indictment of America. But it is also an indictment of the mainstream media. As far as I know no European mainstream newspaper, magazine, TV programme or radio programme has drawn attention to what American scientists and doctors are now doing.

515

Among the cheap 'foods' fed to cattle and pigs on farms in the USA are: human sewage sludge, dead cats and dogs, chicken manure, slaughterhouse waste (blood, bones, intestines), cement kiln dust, old newspapers, waste cardboard, agricultural waste (corn cobs, fruit and vegetable peelings) and old fat from restaurants and grease traps.

516

Every year around 100,000 Americans die because of infections they have caught in hospital. That is over 30 times as many as died in the now infamous 11th September tragedy.

517

Remember: it is true that Saddam Hussein used chemical weapons in his war on Iran. America knew he had the weapons. The ones they didn't give him they gave him the money to buy.

518

One in 20 Americans will spend part of their life in prison.

519

The Americans spent $3 billion a year on surgery for aching knees and then discovered that knee surgery appears to be a waste of time and money.

520

'The Gulf War win in 1991 was one of history's most impressive battlefield achievements, on a par with Agincourt or even Alexander the Great at Issus. But what our military has done in Afghanistan is even more extraordinary.'
DELUDED USA PRESIDENTIAL CANDIDATE STEVE FORBES,
WRITING IN *FORBES GLOBAL* MAGAZINE

521

'It is now clear that the anthrax panic in the UK was entirely unfounded. The anthrax letters in the USA were almost certainly sent by an aggrieved American. The British Government created a crisis and a national panic out of absolutely nothing. I suspect the Government deliberately created a panic to support their 21st century crusade. And I think the British Government did the same thing again when they sent tanks to protect Heathrow. Creating stunts to scare the electors is not what Governments should do.'
READER'S LETTER

522

There are just three countries in the world which impose the death penalty on killers who have such low IQs that they are officially 'mentally retarded'.

The three barbaric, primitive countries on this short list of shame are: Krygyzstan, Japan and the United States of America.

523

It is now common for boys in American schools to be diagnosed as hyperactive. This seems to be particularly likely to happen when the teachers involved are female. Some American schools have abolished recess (playtime) because boys tend to 'run around and shout' and their parents, usually their fathers, have refused to medicate them.

(It is alarming to realise that in the USA boys who run around and shout are regarded by educated and presumably reasonably intelligent professional people as needing medication. What happens in the USA today will probably happen in the rest of the world tomorrow.)

It has been claimed that up to 12 per cent of all American boys aged between 6 and 14 are now being prescribed Ritalin to treat various behavioural disorders. It is not unknown for schools to arrange for children to be treated with Ritalin without obtaining parental permission.

It is worth remembering that although American doctors, parents and teachers have for over thirty years been enthusiastically recommending the use of Ritalin (and similar drugs) there are still a number of unanswered questions.

We still do not know whether the drug works and nor do we know whether it causes any permanent long-term damage. And, perhaps most astonishing of all, despite the fact that millions of children have been diagnosed as suffering from various forms of hyperactivity, and treated with powerful drugs, we do not even know whether any of these conditions really exist.

524

'Superbugs' that are now killing people around the world first appeared in America where antibiotics have for years been wildly overprescribed and used in vast quantities by farmers anxious to boost up the bulk, and therefore the market value, of their animals. (In America over half of all the antibiotics sold are fed to healthy animals). The problem first became clear when it was noticed that the percentage of staphylococci infections resistant to penicillin had risen from 13 per cent in 1960 to 91 per cent in 1988.

To begin with, the new superbugs only caused problems within hospitals – where they caused many deaths among patients whose immune systems had been compromised by other diseases or by physical or mental stresses.

However, by the early 1990s, the staphylococcal superbugs were appearing both inside and outside hospitals all around the world. The problem was so great that the extra costs incurred when doctors had to prescribe increasingly expensive antibiotics was beginning to add an enormous burden to all those responsible for providing health care facilities.

In America, the extra cost of dealing with antibiotic resistant organisms was, as long ago as the end of the 1980s, estimated at being in excess of $30 billion a year. The dollar cost will now be significantly greater than that. The human cost is inestimable.

Doctors in America continue to overprescribe antibiotics and farmers continue to give antibiotics to their animals in order to increase the animals' bulk and their profits.

525

'The way the Americans are treating their prisoners of war in Camp X-ray in Cuba is utterly disgraceful. The prisoners there are held without charge, and without any legal rights. If another country held Americans prisoner in such circumstances the Americans would be hysterical. (And, just out of curiosity, why are the Americans holding their prisoners in Cuba?).'
READER'S LETTER

526

'For N.A.S.A., space is still a high priority.'
GEORGE W. BUSH, PRESIDENT OF THE USA, FORGETTING TO SAY
EXACTLY WHAT ELSE IT IS THAT N.A.S.A. DOES WITH ITS MONEY.

527

As the years have gone by the number of vaccines available has increased steadily. Modern American children receive around thirty vaccinations by the time they go to school. Doctors in other countries are now being encouraged to follow the American example.

Using genetic engineering, there are plans to develop bananas which 'protect' against hepatitis B, measles, yellow fever and poliomyelitis and a genetically engineered potato has been developed which it may be possible to use as a vaccine against cholera. The active part of the potato remains active during the process of cooking and so a portion of genetically engineered chips could soon be a vaccine against cholera.

Naturally, the American drug industry is constantly searching for more and more new vaccines. I have lost count of the number of times I have read of researchers working on a vaccine to prevent cancer. Every year new flu jabs appear on the market. There are vaccines in the pipeline for just about everything ranging from asthma to earache.

There is a planned genetically engineered vaccine which will provide protection against forty different diseases. The vaccine, which will contain the raw DNA of all those different diseases, will be given to newborn babies to provide them with protection for life.

Does anyone know which vaccines are very dangerous and which are just a bit dangerous – and to whom? Does anyone know which vaccines might work a bit and which don't seem to do much good at all? Does anyone know what happens inside the body when all these different vaccinations are given together? Do different vaccines work with or against one another? What about the risk of interactions? Exactly how does the immune system cope when it is suddenly bombarded with so much foreign material?

(There is more about the possible hazards of vaccines and vaccination in my book *Superbody*.)

528

'The Americans get attacked because of their imperialism, their aggressiveness and their unfair trade practices. And yet Britain's taxes go up to help pay for wars the Americans choose to fight against countries (such as Afghanistan) which are not responsible for the attacks America has suffered and which are absolutely no threat to us or to them. I'm afraid I simply don't understand.'
READER'S LETTER

529

An insect called a 'corn borer' costs American farmers around $1 billion a year. So Americans were excited when a genetic engineering company produced a variety of corn which killed the corn borer. The toxin that the new corn produced to kill the insect rather resembled a substance which triggers allergies in some people and that was a bit of a downer. But the developers got round this potential problem by promising to sell the stuff only to farmers who agreed not to sell it to anyone for use in food for humans.

The corn was called Starlink and it was sold by a company now owned by giant drug company Aventis. Farmers loved the stuff. Corn borer killer seeds were quickly planted on 350,000 American acres. But things went wrong (as they usually do) and after being on the market for just three years the modified corn started showing up in all sorts of foods. How dangerous will the new seed turn out to be? Does anyone care? Will this extraordinary story put a stop to the genetic engineering of food?

The answers are: 'no one knows', 'not much' and 'no'.

Around 60 per cent of the soya grown in the USA is already genetically modified and the battle against genetic engineering is lost. All America can do now is wait for the problems to arise and for the lawyers to start circling.

Meanwhile, however, the rest of the world is still trying to stand firm against genetically engineered food. India has frozen food-aid shipments of genetically engineered corn and soy from the USA And, even though three million of its citizens are starving, Zambia turned away 18,000 tons of corn from the USA 'I'd rather die than eat something toxic,' said Zambian president Levy Mwanawasa.

530

'Quite frankly, teachers are the only profession that teach our children.'
GEORGE W. BUSH PROVING ONCE AGAIN HIS INTELLECTUAL DEPTH.

531

A survey in the USA showed that nearly half of all Americans think that human beings were created by God within the last 10,000 years. (They probably also think that God was American, a burger-eating Country & Western fan and lived in Texas.) Even more extraordinary is the fact that a quarter of American college graduates – who, one might have assumed to be a little better educated – also believe that humans were created by God within the last 10,000 years.

532

Every year 180,000 people die in American hospitals because of errors made by doctors or nurses. American hospitals are certainly not places people should visit when sick.

533

'Why did George W. Bush addressing American troops preparing to set off to destroy Iraq remind me of Adolf Hitler addressing his own enthusiastic faithful at a Nuremburg rally?'
READER'S LETTER

534

To say that Bush 'n' Blair are well-intentioned is like saying that Hitler was a compassionate man.

535

'American arrogance seems to have no boundaries. The Americans have consistently refused to do anything at all to control the way they pollute the world. And they don't give a fig for the fact that the rest of the world is suffering as a result of the global warming (and other problems) created largely by their gross over-consumption of energy. Meanwhile, they expect, and demand the rest of the world to support their absurdly aggressive attacks on other countries. George W. Bush is the most dangerous leader in the world. He is a serious threat to world peace.'

READER'S LETTER

536

I was puzzled about why Blair seemed to have 'sold' the UK to Bush. I simply didn't understand why the UK had agreed to help America bomb Afghanistan. And then I discovered that shortly after the bombing started the USA had announced an arms deal with the UK worth approximately £27,000,000,000. Arms deals are a common way to 'launder' money between countries – and to pay for favours. And America is accustomed to 'buying' international support for its selfish policies. Blair and his Chancellor (Brown) know that if they are to win the next election they need to keep tax rises down to a minimum. And yet their incompetence and extravagance means that the UK is running short of cash. The arms deal with the USA will help solve their problem. Simple, selfish, immoral and typically New Labour.

537

Bizarrely and improbably (and with a typical arrogance and ignorance of history) Americans now claim that they gave the English language to the world. There is something curiously satisfying about the fact that the richest, most powerful, most arrogant, most conceited and most brutal nation in the world doesn't even have its own language.

538

The 2003 war against Iraq started on the 3rd March 2003 when USA and UK planes attacked Iraqi installations to destroy weapons which might be used against invading USA forces. The Iraqis claimed six civilians had been killed. The American Government at first admitted that the war had effectively started. The British Government denied it. And within hours the war had apparently stopped again. The attack and the deaths weren't mentioned again.

539

'It isn't pollution that's harming the environment. It's the impurities in our air and water that are doing it.'
GEORGE W. BUSH, PRESIDENT OF THE USA, BUT NO SCIENTIST.

540

'Neither the Americans nor the British seem to realise how widespread the anti-American feeling is. And now that the initial sympathy for the horrors of September 11th is beginning to fade the anti-American feeling is coming to the fore again. 'Pourquoi nous sommes tous anti-americains' was the headline in a major French magazine in late October. All around the world newspapers are explaining their dislike of American arrogance, loudness, tactlessness, selfishness and cheap, plastic culture. In their arrogance the Americans think they are disliked because the rest of the world is jealous of

their wealth. I wish, for their sake and for the world's sake, that the problem was that simple.'
READER'S LETTER

541

'The CIA should turn the crack industry over to General Motors. They'd mismanage the whole thing. Crack would disappear from America in five years.'
MICHAEL MOORE, AUTHOR OF *STUPID WHITE MEN*

542

For me nothing summed up the way America failed to understand the rest of the world better than a picture in *Fortune* magazine which was dated 17 September 2001 but which was, I suspect, put together prior to 11th September. The photograph, from *Fortune* May 1951, showed a building being demolished and was accompanied by this caption: 'The methodical, almost loving destruction of a building seems to answer a deep human need and is surely akin to humour, to impudence, and to the balm of irreverence. Hence the rapt sidewalk attendance at spectacles of demolition. Who has not cheered the loosening of a dignified old cornice? Or glowed inwardly over the nicely calculated fall of a really solid brick wall?'

Only an American magazine, unaware of the pain of blitzes and terrorist bombs, could have printed that. But, I suspect, they won't do it again.

543

After several months of heavy bombing of Afghanistan by the American military, an American 'harmburger' chain announced that it intended to develop 'restaurants' in the destroyed country. Talk about adding insult to injury.

544

George W. Bush, USA president has been arrested three times.

He has been arrested for theft, for disorderly conduct and for drunk driving. How far would you trust a man who has been arrested three times for serious offences? Bush is a recidivist and in the UK wouldn't get permission to have a shotgun licence. But the American people (well, 24 per cent of them) have given him the power to use nuclear weapons.

545

Violence has become a part of everyday life in America. Drive-by shootings and snipers are endemic. People are routinely mugged – and killed – for their small change.

546

Seven billion chickens are raised and killed every year in the USA. An expert working at the University of Georgia has pointed out that just seven chickens produce as much manure as one human being. It is perhaps not surprising that the annual production of animal excrement in the USA now totals in excess of 1.5 billion tons. Altogether, farm animals in America produce ten times as much waste as the human population.

Getting rid of this enormous quantity of excrement obviously poses something of a problem to farmers. You simply can't spread it all on the fields as fertiliser. (Though farmers do get rid of some of the excrement by dumping it onto the land and this is one reason why drinking water supplies in the USA are so polluted.)

So, in an attempt to get rid of all this toxic waste, farmers now frequently mix animal waste into livestock feed. Chicken litter is particularly commonly dealt with in this way, partly because its composition makes it easier to deal with and partly because the quantity of it make its disposal a real problem.

In some areas of America, roughly one in every five chicken

farmers use their chicken manure for cattle feed. Such laws as there are only seem to apply to commercial feed manufacturers and so farmers who keep both chicken and cattle seem to be able to feed chicken manure to cows with impunity.

547

In one recent year, the USA lost 1.43 million jobs but gained 115,000 new managers and executives. There are now 20,300,000 managers and executives working in American industry. This means there is currently one boss for every six workers.

548

Americans claim to want to defend free speech and freedom of assembly but they are the first to make cynical commercial alliances with regimes and industries which oppress their own citizens and employees. American corporations are enthusiastic trade partners with China where freedom is still something of a theoretical concept.

Chinese authorities recently arrested 30 people for using the internet to share information and a former Chinese police officer was sentenced to 11 years imprisonment for downloading articles from pro-democracy web sites.

549

'After the September 11th tragedy, why did people raise money to send to America, the richest nation on earth? Have Americans ever raised money to send to Britons who have suffered at the hands of the IRA? Americans, whose insurance policies provide terrorist cover, can claim for their losses (which will, in part, be paid for by British policyholders) but Britons can claim nothing.'
READER'S LETTER

550

When France and Germany appeared likely to vote against the USA at a United Nations Security Council meeting, American politicians argued that the USA should punish them and bring them into line with 'economic sanctions'. The USA tried to bully or bribe other UN Security Council members. Such blatant jury nobbling would not be accepted in an ordinary courtroom.

551

'The USA claims to believe in, and champion, freedom. Nothing could be further from the truth. The USA has long been an enthusiastic supporter of regimes which stand for oppression and which suppress freedom, privacy and human rights. America's constant concern with its own commercial interests mean that it supports regimes which are cruel, oppressive and uncaring.'
READER'S LETTER

552

In the last ten years the Americans have wasted $150 billion fighting (and losing) their drugs war. Other countries have wasted similarly ludicrous amounts. Since 1980 the number of people in American prisons on drug offences has risen dramatically. The cost of looking after a prisoner is approximately the same as the cost of paying for room, board and tuition for a student at college.

553

An astonishing 20,125 American doctors are reported to be facing disciplinary action. One doctor is accused of using an amputated foot in a crab trap. Another is charged with cutting into the wrong side of a patient's brain.

554

'Multinational corporations employ child labour in order to keep down their prices for rich Americans. The war against Iraq was fought to keep oil prices down. The destruction of Kosovo was organised to please the Americans. The Lockerbie crash was covered up to please the Americans. The American based multinationals constantly get labour concessions and government hand-outs by threatening to move their factories to other parts of the world. The drug companies, for example, only have to drop a hint that they will move an operation from one country to another (relatively easy for them to do) to get governments bending over backwards to reduce taxes and weaken regulations.'
READER'S LETTER

555

The revising of World War II history continues as Americans attempt to disguise their national cowardice and incompetence. For decades American film-makers have made a seemingly endless series of films claiming that just about every World War II battle was won by American servicemen. Americans insult British servicemen with a film about the liberation of the Greek Island of Symi. The film tells the allegedly 'true' story of how USA Commandos battled Nazi troops with the aid of a handful of monks.

The truth is rather different.

In reality the Americans didn't arrive on the island until 1946 when the war was already over. The battle was won by SAS and Special Boat Service members, helped by Greek Orthodox monks.

In recent years American writers and film-makers have made a series of absurd, deeply offensive, boastful and utterly dishonest claims – suggesting that America won World War I and World War II virtually single handed. The result of American self-aggrandisement is that to new generations around the world it must seem as though Britons, Australians and others did nothing much in either of these wars.

Many young Americans actually believe that America helped save the world. In reality, of course, America has never won a war and only took part in World War I and World War II towards the end. America constantly spurned Churchill's requests for help, made a fortune out of ripping off the UK, and only took part in World War II when they had no choice because Germany had declared war on them. American servicemen played a relatively small part in World War II.

556

Following America's example, all countries now classify their enemies as terrorists. Many dictators have found that this is an excellent way to silence freedom fighters and to clamp down on free speech.

557

Evangelical Christians believe that the Second Coming and the City of God are impossible without the state of Israel. The USA is now swamped with right wing Christians of various types. A poll conducted by *Time* magazine showed that nearly two thirds of Americans believe that the book of Revelations will come true. Around a quarter of all Americans believe that the Bible predicted the September 11th attacks.

558

Every year the Americans use up more of the world's energy than France, Germany, India, Japan, Russia and the United Kingdom combined.

559

'I stand by all the misstatements that I've made.'
GEORGE W. BUSH, PRESIDENT OF THE USA, STANDING BY
EVERYTHING HE'S SAID.

560

American fast food chains now have 100,000 restaurants outside the USA selling high fat, high cancer risk food such as 'harmburgers'.

561

It has been clear for years that most of America's military (and quasi military) campaigns in Africa, Asia and Central America simply destabilised the countries involved and led directly to brutal revolutions and civil wars. The amazing thing is that America never seems to learn from its mistakes. One can only put this down to immense arrogance and unquestioning self- belief.

562

'Your some time ago prediction (I think it originally appeared in your book Spiritpower) that the future would be Muslim looks more and more convincing with each passing month. The Americans are creating for themselves (and the rest of the West) a hugely powerful enemy for the future.'
READER'S LETTER

563

War brings out the worst in politicians. The bizarre and utterly dishonest NATO operation in Kosovo is still hailed as a success. After a 78 day aerial bombardment in 1999 the American government claimed that NATO had taken out 120 tanks, 220 armoured personnel carriers and 450 artillery and mortar pieces. However, a suppressed USA Air Force report shows that the accurate count was 14 tanks, 18 armoured personnel carriers and 20 artillery pieces. It is now pretty well clear that NATO did more damage and killed far more innocent people than the 'forces of evil' they were there to suppress.

564

Since the agreed cease fire (dated February 28th 1991) the Americans have continued to attack Iraq – usually sending combat aircraft to attack Iraqi defence installations. These attacks have been carried out quite illegally and without United Nations approval.

565

'America is a very efficient killing machine,' said one American military expert. He's right. Unfortunately, the Americans don't often kill the people they are trying to kill. They have a tendency to bomb refugee trains, surrendering troops, hospitals, allied soldiers, foreign embassies and so on.

566

'The first panacea for a mismanaged nation is inflation of the currency; the second is war. Both bring a temporary prosperity; both bring a permanent ruin. But both are the refuge of political and economic opportunists.'
ERNEST HEMINGWAY

567

George W. Bush and Tony Blair have claimed that they had to attack Iraq to protect the USA and the UK. The implication is that if they had been leading their countries in the 1930s they would have attacked Germany to prevent World War II.

Have they forgotten that when Germany attacked Poland, Hitler claimed that he was attacking pre-emptively, in order to defend Germany from a forthcoming attack from Poland?

Bush 'n' Blair are now using exactly the same argument that was used by Hitler. They are now the bad guys.

568

'There is no instance of a country having benefited from prolonged warfare.'
SUN TZU, *THE ART OF WAR*

569

The American government was warned that an attack on Iraq could lead to civil wars in Egypt, Jordan and Saudi Arabia. The American response was: 'So what?' The Americans believe that countries in the Middle East are out of touch with Western, Christian values. Astonishingly, the Americans genuinely seem to believe that uprisings in the Middle East will lead to the installation of American-style Christian democracies.

570

The American Government constantly says one thing and does another. It imposes standards on the rest of the world which it refuses to accept itself. It has consistently shown a disregard for international law and a contempt for human rights.

The Americans claim to be the fount of goodness but they refuse to do anything to help poor countries – indeed, over the last couple of decades they have introduced policies which have directly led to the deaths of millions of innocent people. America's idea of diplomacy is to carpet bomb countries which upset America.

The Americans deny basic human rights to whole countries and then arrogantly claim that they know best. They insist that price stability within America is more important than the future of the planet; they continue to destroy our environment (as well as their own) and to wage war against innocents all around the world.

Virtually every day there are reports of American hypocrisy. The American president claims that his country leads the world in justice and yet his is the one of the few countries which routinely executes children. American presidents wage war to distract attention from their sexual peccadilloes. They insist that developing countries have properly supervised elections and yet they themselves conduct a presidential election which is decided when the so-called Supreme Court arbitrarily decides not to recount votes which would almost certainly have changed the result of the election.

A headline in an American newspaper ran: 'All Nations on Earth Sign Global Warming Agreement. USA Refuses.' And still they wonder why everyone loathes and despises them.

The Americans expect the rest of the world to worship their flag, but they seem unable to understand that respect has to be earned and cannot simply be demanded. The Americans believe that their definitions are the only ones that count; they believe that if they say that someone is a terrorist then the rest of the world must regard him as a terrorist. The Americans fund terrorists in Ireland but think that the English are being unreasonable if they complain.

The Americans believe that the only form of justice that matters is American justice – even though to the rest of the world American justice doesn't look, sound or smell much like justice at all.

The Americans have a commercial view of human rights. They change their views according to the combatants. The Americans regard China as an important trading partner so they put up with human rights violations there. The Americans need Saudi oil so they turn a blind eye to human rights violations in that country too. But they will carpet bomb Afghanistan and Iraq to force regime changes in those countries.

The Americans claim to respect the freedom of the press and the individual's freedom of speech but they will close down web sites which are critical of America. When Americans closed down my web site the American FBI refused to cooperate with the British police to arrest the criminal involved. But when a British citizen interfered with American web sites the Americans insisted that the British authorities deal with him.

In February 2003, at the same time that they were begging for British support for their latest war on Iraq, the Americans told the South Africans to arrest an innocent British pensioner but then left him in prison for ten days before even bothering to go and interview him.

There is, in American hearts and minds, one rule for Americans and one rule for the rest of the world. The Americans are widely loathed. And the loathing will get worse, much worse, before it gets better.

Americans claim to offer freedom on religious matters but insist that the world convert to Christianity – preferably of the right variety. The Americans regard themselves as missionaries – chosen by God to lead the world. And still they wonder why the world dislikes them.

To Americans, history started just after they stole their nation from the natives. There is no equality of opportunity in the USA but they pretend there is. The American revolution started with the battle-cry 'No taxation without representation'. But the Americans now tax the world – and refuse to allow any representation.

The Americans have handed power to the lobbyists and the public relations specialists. He who has the biggest bank balance has the most power. That is the American version of freedom. Frankly, it stinks.

It is hardly surprising that around the world people distrust America and Americans. It is hardly surprising that very few non-Americans have much confidence or faith in America.

The Americans steal, corrupt and pollute without a thought for the rest of the world. They are contemptuous and condescending, greedy and uncaring. They refuse to accept international laws on how to deal with prisoners of war. They demand immunity from the war crimes court for their own soldiers. They are by far the world's biggest polluter but they refuse to ratify the Kyoto Treaty because it may damage their own internal economy. They steal and patent seeds and plants and then sell those seeds and plants back to starving people in developing countries. They foist genetically engineered products on a world which doesn't want them. They claim to worship capitalism and freedom and yet the American government owns nearly 40 per cent of all land in the USA.

The greed and dishonesty of corporate employees in America has been a primary factor in helping to push the world economy into recession. And still they wonder why the rest of the world dislikes them.

The Americans think they are disliked because they are rich. They are wrong. Very wrong. They are disliked, in part, because of the way they got rich and because of the way they now behave.

571

'It is time for the human race to enter the solar system.'
GEORGE W. BUSH, PRESIDENT OF THE USA.

VERNON COLEMAN

Afterword

My original title for this book was 'Why The World Hates America'.
But then I remembered that a few years ago, when I had used that
title for an article on America, a very good friend of mine (born an
American) questioned my use of the word 'hate'. He pointed out
that the word would antagonise and polarise Americans and,
perhaps, prevent them from even reading what I had written, or
listening to what I was trying to tell them.

He was right, of course.

It is perfectly true that much of the world does hate America,
but if those of us who are appalled by American behaviour are
ever to persuade the Americans to change their ways, to treat other
countries with respect and to start obeying international laws, we
must first persuade them to listen to what we have to say.

In addition, of course, we must spread the truth about America
to those people living outside the USA. There are millions of
people around the world who now only receive information via
American owned media outlets; their only view of America is
derived from American owned print media, from American
television programmes and from American movies.

If you have found this book informative please pass it on to
someone whom you think would benefit from reading it – whether
they live in or outside America. (If someone gave you this book to
read please thank them for me.)

My purpose in writing this book is not to attack America: it is to
try to save the world from America and to help Americans save
themselves. At the moment America is dragging us all, at break-
neck speed, towards oblivion. The oblivion may come quickly, as
an American inspired version of Armageddon, or slowly, with the
world being destroyed by America's refusal to do anything about
problems such as global warming.

If you would like more copies of *Rogue Nation* to distribute please
get in touch with Blue Books at Publishing House. We are making
bulk purchase copies of this book available at specially reduced
prices for readers who would like to help spread the word.

Vernon Coleman, 2003

For a catalogue of Vernon Coleman's books
please write to:

Publishing House
Trinity Place
Barnstaple
Devon EX32 9HJ
England

Telephone   01271 328892
Fax   01271 328768

Outside the UK:
Telephone   +44 1271 328892
Fax   +44 1271 328768

Or visit our website:

www.vernoncoleman.com